SUPREME COURT WATCH 2009

Highlights of the 2007 and 2008 Terms
Preview of the 2009 Term

DAVID M. O'BRIEN

UNIVERSITY OF VIRGINIA

W • W • **NORTON & COMPANY** • NEW YORK • LONDON

W. W. Norton & Company has been independent since its founding in 1923, when William Warder Norton and Mary D. Herter Norton first published lectures delivered at the People's Institute, the adult education division of New York City's Cooper Union. The firm soon expanded its program beyond the Institute, publishing books by celebrated academics from America and abroad. By midcentury, the two major pillars of Norton's publishing program—trade books and college texts—were firmly established. In the 1950s, the Norton family transferred control of the company to its employees, and today—with a staff of four hundred and a comparable number of trade, college, and professional titles published each year—W. W. Norton & Company stands as the largest and oldest publishing house owned wholly by its employees.

Composition by Cathy Lombardi.
Manufacturing by Courier—Westford.
Production Manager: Ben Reynolds.

ISBN: 978-0-393-93516-5

W. W. Norton & Company, Inc., 500 Fifth Avenue, New York, NY 10110-0017
www.wwnorton.com

W. W. Norton & Company Ltd., Castle House, 75/76 Wells Street,
London W1T 3QT

1 2 3 4 5 6 7 8 9 0

Contents

PREFACE

Supreme Court Watch 2009 examines the changes and decisions made during the Supreme Court's 2007 and 2008 terms. In addition to highlighting the major constitutional rulings in excerpts from leading cases, I discuss in section-by-section introductions other important decisions and analyze recent developments in various areas of constitutional law. The important cases that the Court has granted review and will decide in its 2009–2010 term are also previewed. To offer even more information in an efficient format, special boxes titled "The Development of Law" and "In Comparative Perspective" are also included.

The favorable reception of previous editions of the *Watch* has been gratifying, and I hope that this nineteenth edition will further contribute to students' understanding of constitutional law, politics, and history, as well as to their appreciation for how the politics of constitutional interpretation turns on differing interpretations of constitutional politics and the role of the Supreme Court. I am most grateful to Aaron Javsicas for doing a terrific and expeditious job in producing this edition.

D.M.O.
July 1, 2009

SUPREME COURT WATCH 2009

VOLUME ONE

2

LAW AND POLITICS IN THE SUPREME COURT: JURISDICTION AND DECISION-MAKING PROCESS

Continuing a decade-old trend, in its 2007 and 2008 terms the Court granted and decided by written opinions less than 1 percent of its total docket of almost 10,000 cases (see the "Inside the Court" boxes in this chapter). In its 2007 term the docket fell slightly from the prior term of over 10,000 cases to 9, 602 cases. Still, the Court heard oral arguments and decided less than 80 cases. As usual, the Court more often reversed than affirmed the decisions below, as indicated in the following table.

On April 30, 2009, Justice Souter, at age 69, announced that he would retire after eighteen terms on the Court. President Barak Obama anticipated filling one or more vacancies on the high bench even before his election, and in December directed a small group of White House staff to begin the process of narrowing the pool of potential nominees. In mid-April the administration learned privately that Justice Souter intended to retire at the end of the term and staff—led by White House Counsel Gregory B. Craig and Ronald A. Klain and Cynthia Hogan of Vice President Joseph R. Biden's office—began assembling more names and reviewing their backgrounds. From a pool of about forty potential nominees, the list was narrowed to nine and, then, to a final four—Second Circuit Court of Appeals Judge Sonia Sotomayor, Seventh Circuit Court of Appeals Judge Diane P. Wood, Solicitor General Elena Kagan, and Homeland Security Secretary Janet Napolitano—all of whom the president subsequently met with in the Oval Office. Although he knew Judge Wood from their days teaching at the University of Chicago, and appointed Kagan and Napolitano to positions in his administration, Obama had not met Judge Sotomayor until an interview on May 21, 2009. President Obama then announced her nomination on May 26th, observing that she would bring a diversity of experience to the Court and had a compelling personal background and an impressive legal record. Judge Sotomayor, age 54, grew up in the Bronx, the daughter of immigrants from Puerto Rico and then went to Princeton University and Yale Law School, where she was an editor of the *Yale Law Journal*. After spending five years as a prosecutor in Manhattan and then working in private practice, she was appointed in 1992 to the federal district court by Republican President George H. W. Bush upon the recommendation of Democratic Senator Daniel Patrick Moynihan, and later elevated to the Court of Appeals for the Second Circuit by Democratic President Bill Clinton in 1998. In announcing her nomination, President Obama aimed to receive the Democratically-controlled Senate's confirmation by the beginning of the Court's term on the first Monday in October. The Senate Judiciary Committee recommended her confirmation by a thirteen to six vote in late July, and in August the full Senate confirmed Sotomayor as the 111th justice, the first Latina, and third female justice to serve on the Court; she would also bring the number of Catholics serving at the same time to six, the highest number in the history of the Court.

The Court's Disposition of Appeals in the 2008 Term

	AFFIRMED	REVERSED OR VACATED
First Circuit	2	2
Second Circuit	3	6
Third Circuit	1	1
Fourth Circuit		4
Fifth Circuit	2	3
Sixth Circuit		5
Seventh Circuit		2
Eighth Circuit		4
Ninth Circuit	2	15
Tenth Circuit		2
Eleventh Circuit	2	1
Federal Circuit		4
District of Columbia Circuit		1
Other Federal Courts		1
State Courts and Other	4	11
*Totals:	16	62

*Excludes cases decided on original jurisdiction or dismissed for lack of jurisdiction and remanded.

B | *The Court's Docket and Screening Cases*

■ INSIDE THE COURT

The Business of the Supreme Court in the 2008–2009 Term★

SUBJECT OF COURT OPINIONS	SUMMARY	PLENARY
Admiralty		1
Antitrust		1
Bankruptcy		1
Bill of Rights (other than rights of accused) and Equal Protection		3
Commerce Clause		
1. Constitutionality and construction of federal regulation		2
2. Constitutionality of state regulation		1
Common Law		
Miscellaneous Statutory Construction	1	24
Due process		
1. Economic interests		
2. Procedure and rights of accused		13
3. Substantive due process (noneconomic)		1
Impairment of Contract and Just Compensation		
International Law, War, and Peace		1
Jurisdiction, Procedure, and Practice	5	18
Land Legislation		1
Native Americans		2
Patents, Copyright, and Trademarks		
Other Suits against the Government		3
Suits by States		1
Taxation (federal and state)		1
Totals	6	74

★Note: The classification of cases is that of the author and necessarily invites differences of opinion as to the dominant issue in some cases. The table includes opinions in cases whether decided summarily or given plenary consideration, but not cases summarily disposed of by simple orders, opinions dissenting from the denial of review, and those dismissing cases as improvidently granted.

H | *Opinion Days and Communicating Decisions*

■ INSIDE THE COURT

*Opinion Writing during the 2008–2009 Term**

OPINIONS	MAJORITY	CONCURRING	DISSENTING	SEPARATE	TOTALS
Per Curiam	7				7
Roberts	8	3	2	1	14
Stevens	9	3	13	2	27
Scalia	11	6	3	1	21
Kennedy	6	4	1	1	12
Souter	8	2	10	1	21
Thomas	9	4	5	2	20
Ginsburg	7	1	9	1	18
Breyer	8	6	11	3	28
Alito	7	9	6	1	23
Totals	80	38	60	13	191

*Note that court opinions disposing of two or more companion cases are counted only once here. In addition, this table includes opinions in cases disposed of either summarily or upon plenary consideration, but does not include cases summarily disposed of by simple orders, dismissed as improvidently granted, and concurring or dissenting opinions from the denial of *certiorari*.

I | *Impact of Supreme Court Decisions: Compliance and Implementation*

The Roberts Court, again, reconsidered the doctrine of retroactivity of its decisions, established in *Linkletter v. Walker*, 381 U.S. 618 (1965) (excerpted in Vols. 1 and 2, Ch. 2), *Griffith v. Kentucky*, 479 U.S. 314 (1987) (excerpted in Vols. 1 and 2, Ch. 2), and *Teague v. Lane*, 489 U.S. 288 (1989). Under *Teague*, an old ruling applies both on direct and collateral review, but a new rule, overturning a precedent, applies only to cases still on direct review and applies retroactively in collateral proceedings only if (1) it is substantive or (2) a watershed ruling bearing on "the fundamental fairness and accuracy of the criminal proceeding." In *Whorton v. Bockting*, 549 U.S. 406 (2007), writing for a unanimous Court, Justice Alito reaffirmed *Teague* in holding that a new ruling, which is neither substantive nor a watershed, does not apply retroactively to cases on collateral review in federal courts. However, in *Danforth v. Minnesota*, 128 S.Ct. 1029 (2008), Justice Stevens held that under *Teague* state courts were free to apply broader retroactivity, observing that *Teague* serves to "limit the authority of federal courts to overturn state convictions—not to limit a state court's authority to grant relief for violations of new rules of constitutional law when reviewing its own state convictions." Chief Justice Roberts dissented.

3

PRESIDENTIAL POWER,
THE RULE OF LAW,
AND FOREIGN AFFAIRS

C | *The Treaty-Making Power and*
| *Executive Independence*

In its 2007–2008 term, the Roberts Court rebuffed President George W. Bush's broad assertion of executive power with respect to the enforcement of interpretations of treaty provisions. In 2004, the International Court of Justice (ICJ) ruled against the denial of certain procedural rights under provisions of the Vienna Convention. Subsequently, President Bush issued a memorandum directing Texas state courts to comply with the ICJ's decision, but they balked and held that the president exceeded his constitutional authority over the conduct of foreign affairs and intruded on the independence of state court proceedings. On appeal in *Medellin v. Texas* (2008) (excerpted below), six members of the Court rejected the administration's interpretation of the Vienna Convention and position on presidential power. Writing for the majority, Chief Justice Roberts held that the convention was a non-self-executing treaty, requiring further congressional legislation to make the ICJ's ruling binding on domestic courts; in contrast to self-executing treaties that have immediate binding legal effect. In addition, he held that President Bush's order had no binding legal effect because it exceeded his authority under the treaty-making provision of the Constitution. Non-self-executing treaties require congressional legislation to force interpretations of their provisions. Thus, neither the ICJ's decision nor President Bush's memorandum, in the absence of federal legislation, compelled state courts to alter their procedures for granting writs of *habeas corpus*. Justice Stevens filed a concurring opinion. Justice Breyer issued a dissenting opinion, which Justices Souter and Ginsburg joined, countering that the Vienna Convention was a self-executing treaty and had binding legal effect.

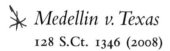

Medellin v. Texas
128 S.Ct. 1346 (2008)

Jose Medellin was convicted of murder and sentenced to death in Texas. He filed in state courts for a writ of *habeas corpus*, contending that he had a right as a foreign national to consult Mexican authorities, under the Vienna Convention on Consular Relations, and he had not been informed of that right at his trial. After his appeal was dismissed, Mexico filed a suit against the United States in the International Court of Justice (ICJ), which has jurisdiction over disputes arising from the convention and other treaties. Mexico contended that Medellin and fifty other Mexican nationals had been denied their procedural rights under the treaty. The ICJ, in the *Case Concerning Avena and Other Mexican Nationals (Mex. v. U.S.)*, 2004 I.C.J. 12 (*Avena*), held that the nationals were entitled to reconsideration of their convictions and sentences in the United States.

Medellin appealed his conviction, relying on the ICJ's *Avena* ruling. But a federal appellate court dismissed his petition, holding that he was procedurally barred from *habeas* relief because he had not raised the claim during his original trial. He in turn appealed that decision and his death sentence to the Supreme Court. While the Court was considering his appeal, in February 2005 President George W. Bush issued a memorandum announcing that the United States would comply with *Avena* "by having state courts give effect to the [ICJ] decision in accordance with general principles of comity filed by the 51 Mexican nationals addressed in that decision." Subsequently, the Court by a five-to-four vote dismissed Medellin's appeal in an unsigned decision to allow Texas courts to comply with the presidential memorandum. Medellin once again appealed to the Texas courts, contending that they should comply with the ICJ's ruling and Bush's memorandum. But in 2006 the Texas Court of Criminal Appeals dismissed his petition and held that the ICJ's ruling was not binding on state courts. The state appellate court also held that President Bush exceeded his constitutional authority over foreign affairs and intruded on the independent powers of state courts. Medellin, again, appealed to the Supreme Court, which granted review.

The state appellate court's decision was affirmed by a six-to-three vote. Chief Justice Roberts delivered the opinion for the Court. Justice Stevens filed a concurring opinion. Justice Breyer issued a dissenting opinion, which Justices Souter and Ginsburg joined.

☐ *CHIEF JUSTICE ROBERTS delivered the opinion of the Court.*

The International Court of Justice (ICJ), located in the Hague, is a tribunal established pursuant to the United Nations Charter to adjudicate disputes between member states. In the *Case Concerning Avena and Other Mexican Nationals (Mex. v. U.S.)*, 2004 I. C. J. 12 (Judgment of Mar. 31) (*Avena*), that tribunal considered a claim brought by Mexico against the United States. The ICJ held that, based on violations of the Vienna Convention, 51 named Mexican nationals were entitled to review and reconsideration of their state-court convictions and sentences in the United States. This was so regardless of any forfeiture of the right to raise Vienna Convention claims because of a failure to comply with generally applicable state rules governing challenges to criminal convictions.

In *Sanchez-Llamas v. Oregon*, 548 U.S. 331 (2006)—issued after *Avena* but involving individuals who were not named in the *Avena* judgment—we held that, contrary to the ICJ's determination, the Vienna Convention did not preclude the application of state default rules. After the *Avena* decision, President George W. Bush determined, through a Memorandum to the Attorney General (Feb. 28, 2005), (Memorandum or President's Memorandum), that the United States would "discharge its international obligations" under *Avena* "by having State courts give effect to the decision." . . .

In 1969, the United States, upon the advice and consent of the Senate, ratified the Vienna Convention on Consular Relations (Vienna Convention or Convention), the Optional Protocol Concerning the Compulsory Settlement of Disputes to the Vienna Convention (Optional Protocol or Protocol). . . . Art. 36(1) provides that if a person detained by a foreign country "so requests, the competent authorities of the receiving State shall, without delay, inform the consular post of the sending State" of such detention, and "inform the [detainee] of his righ[t]" to request assistance from the consul of his own state. . . .

Under Article 94(1) of the U.N. Charter, "[e]ach Member of the United Nations undertakes to comply with the decision of the [ICJ] in any case to which it is a party." The ICJ's jurisdiction in any particular case, however, is dependent upon the consent of the parties. The ICJ Statute delineates two ways in which a nation may consent to ICJ jurisdiction: It may consent generally to jurisdiction on any question arising under a treaty or general international law, or it may consent specifically to jurisdiction over a particular category of cases or disputes pursuant to a separate treaty. The United States originally consented to the general jurisdiction of the ICJ when it filed a declaration recognizing compulsory jurisdiction under Art. 36(2) in 1946. The United States withdrew from general ICJ jurisdiction in 1985. By ratifying the Optional Protocol to the Vienna Convention, the United States consented to the specific jurisdiction of the ICJ with respect to claims arising out of the Vienna Convention. On March 7, 2005, subsequent to the ICJ's judgment in *Avena*, the United States gave notice of withdrawal from the Optional Protocol to the Vienna Convention. . . .

Medellin first contends that the ICJ's judgment in *Avena* constitutes a "binding" obligation on the state and federal courts of the United States. He argues that "by virtue of the Supremacy Clause, the treaties requiring compliance with the *Avena* judgment are already the 'Law of the Land' by which all state and federal courts in this country are 'bound.'" Accordingly, Medellin argues, *Avena* is a binding federal rule of decision that pre-empts contrary state limitations on successive *habeas* petitions.

No one disputes that the *Avena* decision—a decision that flows from the treaties through which the United States submitted to ICJ jurisdiction with respect to Vienna Convention disputes—constitutes an international law obligation on the part of the United States. But not all international law obligations automatically constitute binding federal law enforceable in United States courts. The question we confront here is whether the *Avena* judgment has automatic domestic legal effect such that the judgment of its own force applies in state and federal courts.

This Court has long recognized the distinction between treaties that automatically have effect as domestic law, and those that—while they constitute international law commitments—do not by themselves function as binding federal law. The distinction was well explained by CHIEF JUSTICE MARSHALL's opinion in *Foster v. Neilson*, 2 Pet. 253 (1829), overruled on other grounds, *United States v. Percheman*, 7 Pet. 51 (1833), which held that a treaty is "equivalent to an act of the legislature," and hence self-executing, when it "operates of itself without the aid of any legislative provision." When, in contrast, "[treaty] stipulations are not self-executing they can only be enforced pursuant to legislation to carry them into effect." *Whitney v. Robertson*, 124 U.S. 190 (1888). In sum, while treaties "may comprise international commitments . . . they are not domestic law unless Congress has either enacted implementing statutes or the treaty itself conveys an intention that it be 'self-executing' and is ratified on these terms."

A treaty is, of course, "primarily a compact between independent nations." *Head Money Cases*, 112 U.S. 580 (1884). It ordinarily "depends for the enforcement of its provisions on the interest and the honor of the governments which are parties to it." Only "[i]f the treaty contains stipulations which are self-executing, that is, require no legislation to make them operative, [will] they have the force and effect of a legislative enactment." *Whitney*.

The interpretation of a treaty, like the interpretation of a statute, begins with its text. *Air France v. Saks*, 470 U.S. 392 (1985). Because a treaty ratified by the United States is "an agreement among sovereign powers," we have also considered as "aids to its interpretation" the negotiation and drafting history of the treaty as well as "the post ratification understanding" of signatory nations. *Zicherman v. Korean Air Lines Co.*, 516 U.S. 217 (1996).

As a signatory to the Optional Protocol, the United States agreed to submit disputes arising out of the Vienna Convention to the ICJ. The Protocol provides: "Disputes arising out of the interpretation or application of the [Vienna] Convention shall lie within the compulsory jurisdiction of the International Court of Justice." Of course, submitting to jurisdiction and agreeing to be bound are two different things. A party could, for example, agree to compulsory nonbinding arbitration. Such an agreement would require the party to appear before the arbitral tribunal without obligating the party to treat the tribunal's decision as binding.

The most natural reading of the Optional Protocol is as a bare grant of jurisdiction. It provides only that "[d]isputes arising out of the interpretation or application of the [Vienna] Convention shall lie within the compulsory jurisdiction of the International Court of Justice" and "may accordingly be brought before the [ICJ] . . . by any party to the dispute being a Party to the present Protocol." The Protocol says nothing about the effect of an ICJ decision and does not itself commit signatories to comply with an ICJ judgment. The Protocol is similarly silent as to any enforcement mechanism.

The obligation on the part of signatory nations to comply with ICJ judgments derives not from the Optional Protocol, but rather from Article 94 of the United Nations Charter—the provision that specifically addresses the effect of ICJ decisions. Article 94(1) provides that "[e]ach Member of the United Nations undertakes to comply with the decision of the [ICJ] in any case to which it is a party." The Executive Branch contends that the phrase "undertakes to comply" is not "an acknowledgement that an ICJ decision will have immediate legal effect in the courts of U.N. members," but rather "a commitment on the part of U.N. Members to take future action through their political branches to comply with an ICJ decision."

We agree with this construction of Article 94. The Article is not a directive to domestic courts. It does not provide that the United States "shall" or "must" comply with an ICJ decision, nor indicate that the Senate that ratified the U.N. Charter intended to vest ICJ decisions with immediate legal effect in domestic courts. In other words, the U.N. Charter reads like "a compact between independent nations" that "depends for the enforcement of its provisions on the interest and the honor of the governments which are parties to it." *Head Money Cases.*

The remainder of Article 94 confirms that the U.N. Charter does not contemplate the automatic enforceability of ICJ decisions in domestic courts. Article 94(2)—the enforcement provision—provides the sole remedy for noncompliance: referral to the United Nations Security Council by an aggrieved state. . . .

If ICJ judgments were instead regarded as automatically enforceable domestic law, they would be immediately and directly binding on state and federal courts pursuant to the Supremacy Clause. Mexico or the ICJ would have no need to proceed to the Security Council to enforce the judgment in this case. Noncompliance with an ICJ judgment through exercise of the Security Council veto—always regarded as an option by the Executive and ratifying Senate during and after consideration of the U.N. Charter, Optional Protocol, and ICJ Statute—would no longer be a viable alternative. There would be nothing to veto. In light of the U.N. Charter's remedial scheme, there is no reason to believe that the President and Senate signed up for such a result.

In sum, Medellin's view that ICJ decisions are automatically enforceable as domestic law is fatally undermined by the enforcement structure established by Article 94. His construction would eliminate the option of noncompliance contemplated by Article 94(2), undermining the ability of the political branches to determine whether and how to comply with an ICJ judgment. Those sensitive foreign policy decisions would instead be transferred to state and federal courts charged with applying an ICJ judgment directly as domestic law. And those courts would not be empowered to decide whether to comply with the judgment—again, always regarded as an option by the political branches—any more than courts may consider whether to comply with any other species of domestic law. This result would be particularly anomalous in light of the principle that "[t]he conduct of the foreign relations of our Government is committed by the Constitution to the Executive and Legislative—'the political'—Departments." *Oetjen v. Central Leather Co.*, 246 U.S. 297 (1918).

The ICJ Statute, incorporated into the U.N. Charter, provides further evidence that the ICJ's judgment in *Avena* does not automatically constitute federal law judicially enforceable in United States courts. To begin with, the ICJ's "principal purpose" is said to be to "arbitrate particular disputes between national governments." Accordingly, the ICJ can hear disputes only between nations, not individuals. More important, Article 59 of the statute provides that "[t]he decision of the [ICJ] has no binding force except between the parties and in respect of that particular case." The dissent does not explain how Medellín, an individual, can be a party to the ICJ proceeding. . . .

The pertinent international agreements, therefore, do not provide for implementation of ICJ judgments through direct enforcement in domestic courts, and "where a treaty does not provide a particular remedy, either expressly or implicitly, it is not for the federal courts to impose one on the States through lawmaking of their own." . . .

Our Framers established a careful set of procedures that must be followed before federal law can be created under the Constitution—vesting that decision in the political branches, subject to checks and balances. U.S. Const., Art. I, Sec. 7. They also recognized that treaties could create federal law, but again through the political branches, with the President making the treaty and the Senate approving it. Art. II, Sec. 2. The dissent's understanding of the treaty route, depending on an ad hoc judgment of the judiciary without looking to the treaty language—the very language negotiated by the President and approved by the Senate—cannot readily be ascribed to those same Framers.

The dissent's approach risks the United States' involvement in international agreements. It is hard to believe that the United States would enter into treaties that are sometimes enforceable and sometimes not. Such a treaty would be the equivalent of writing a blank check to the judiciary. Senators could never be quite sure what the treaties on which they were voting meant. Only a judge could say for sure and only at some future date. This uncertainty could hobble the United States' efforts to negotiate and sign international agreements.

In this case, the dissent—for a grab bag of no less than seven reasons—would tell us that this particular ICJ judgment is federal law. That is no sort of guidance. Nor is it any answer to say that the federal courts will diligently police international agreements and enforce the decisions of international tribunals only when they should be enforced. The point of a non-self-executing treaty is that it "addresses itself to the political, not the judicial department; and the legislature must execute the contract before it can become a rule for the Court." . . .

Our holding does not call into question the ordinary enforcement of foreign judgments or international arbitral agreements. Indeed, we agree with Medellín that, as a general matter, "an agreement to abide by the result" of an international adjudication—or what he really means, an agreement to give the result of such adjudication domestic legal effect—can be a treaty obligation like any other, so long as the agreement is consistent with the Constitution. The point is that the particular treaty obligations on which Medellín relies do not of their own force create domestic law. . . .

In sum, while the ICJ's judgment in *Avena* creates an international law obligation on the part of the United States, it does not of its own force constitute binding federal law that pre-empts state restrictions on the filing of successive habeas petitions. Nothing in the text, background, negotiating and drafting history, or practice among signatory nations suggests that the President or Senate intended the improbable result of giving the judgments of an international tribunal a higher status than that enjoyed by "many of our most fundamental constitutional protections."

Medellin next argues that the ICJ's judgment in *Avena* is binding on state courts by virtue of the President's February 28, 2005 Memorandum. The United States contends that while the *Avena* judgment does not of its own force require domestic courts to set aside ordinary rules of procedural default, that judgment became the law of the land with precisely that effect pursuant to the President's Memorandum and his power "to establish binding rules of decision that preempt contrary state law." Accordingly, we must decide whether the President's declaration alters our conclusion that the *Avena* judgment is not a rule of domestic law binding in state and federal courts.

The United States maintains that the President's constitutional role "uniquely qualifies" him to resolve the sensitive foreign policy decisions that bear on compliance with an ICJ decision and "to do so expeditiously." In this case, the President seeks to vindicate United States interests in ensuring the reciprocal observance of the Vienna Convention, protecting relations with foreign governments, and demonstrating commitment to the role of international law. These interests are plainly compelling.

Such considerations, however, do not allow us to set aside first principles. The President's authority to act, as with the exercise of any governmental power, "must stem either from an act of Congress or from the Constitution itself." *Youngstown* [*Sheet & Tube v. Sawyer*, 343 U.S. 579 (1952)].

Justice Jackson's familiar tripartite scheme provides the accepted framework for evaluating executive action in this area. First, "[w]hen the President acts pursuant to an express or implied authorization of Congress, his authority is at its maximum, for it includes all that he possesses in his own right plus all that Congress can delegate." *Youngstown*. Second, "[w]hen the President acts in absence of either a congressional grant or denial of authority, he can only rely upon his own independent powers, but there is a zone of twilight in which he and Congress may have concurrent authority, or in which its distribution is uncertain." In this circumstance, Presidential authority can derive support from "congressional inertia, indifference or quiescence." Finally, "[w]hen the President takes measures incompatible with the expressed or implied will of Congress, his power is at its lowest ebb," and the Court can sustain his actions "only by disabling the Congress from acting upon the subject."

The United States marshals' two principal arguments in favor of the President's authority "to establish binding rules of decision that preempt contrary state law." The Solicitor General first argues that the relevant treaties give the President the authority to implement the *Avena* judgment and that Congress has acquiesced in the exercise of such authority. The United States also relies upon an "independent" international dispute-resolution power wholly apart from the asserted authority based on the pertinent treaties. Medellin adds the additional argument that the President's Memorandum is a valid exercise of his power to take care that the laws be faithfully executed.

The United States maintains that the President's Memorandum is authorized by the Optional Protocol and the U.N. Charter. That is, because the relevant treaties "create an obligation to comply with *Avena*," they "implicitly give the President authority to implement that treaty-based obligation." As a result, the President's Memorandum is well grounded in the first category of the *Youngstown* framework.

We disagree. The President has an array of political and diplomatic means available to enforce international obligations, but unilaterally converting a non-self-executing treaty into a self-executing one is not among them. The responsibility for transforming an international obligation arising from a non-self-executing treaty into domestic law falls to Congress. . . .

The requirement that Congress, rather than the President, implement a non-self-executing treaty derives from the text of the Constitution, which divides the treaty-making power between the President and the Senate. The Constitution vests the President with the authority to "make" a treaty. If the Executive determines that a treaty should have domestic effect of its own force, that determination may be implemented "in mak[ing]" the treaty, by ensuring that it contains language plainly providing for domestic enforceability. If the treaty is to be self-executing in this respect, the Senate must consent to the treaty by the requisite two-thirds vote consistent with all other constitutional restraints.

Once a treaty is ratified without provisions clearly according it domestic effect, however, whether the treaty will ever have such effect is governed by the fundamental constitutional principle that "'[t]he power to make the necessary laws is in Congress; the power to execute in the President.'" *Hamdan v. Rumsfeld*, 548 U.S. 557 (2006). As already noted, the terms of a non-self-executing treaty can become domestic law only in the same way as any other law—through passage of legislation by both Houses of Congress, combined with either the President's signature or a congressional override of a Presidential veto. Indeed, "the President's power to see that the laws are faithfully executed refutes the idea that he is to be a lawmaker." *Youngstown*.

A non-self-executing treaty, by definition, is one that was ratified with the understanding that it is not to have domestic effect of its own force. That understanding precludes the assertion that Congress has implicitly authorized the President—acting on his own—to achieve precisely the same result. We therefore conclude, given the absence of congressional legislation, that the non-self-executing treaties at issue here did not "express[ly] or implied[ly]" vest the President with the unilateral authority to make them self-executing. Accordingly, the President's Memorandum does not fall within the first category of the *Youngstown* framework. . . .

The United States nonetheless maintains that the President's Memorandum should be given effect as domestic law because "this case involves a valid Presidential action in the context of Congressional 'acquiescence'." Under the *Youngstown* tripartite framework, congressional acquiescence is pertinent when the President's action falls within the second category—that is, when he "acts in absence of either a congressional grant or denial of authority." Here, however, as we have explained, the President's effort to accord domestic effect to the *Avena* judgment does not meet that prerequisite. . . .

We thus turn to the United States' claim that—independent of the United States' treaty obligations—the Memorandum is a valid exercise of the President's foreign affairs authority to resolve claims disputes with foreign nations. The United States relies on a series of cases in which this Court has upheld the authority of the President to settle foreign claims pursuant to an executive agreement. . . .

This argument is of a different nature than the one rejected above. Rather than relying on the United States' treaty obligations, the President relies on an independent source of authority in ordering Texas to put aside its procedural bar to successive *habeas* petitions. Nevertheless, we find that our claims-settlement cases [*United States v. Pink*, 315 U.S. 202 (1942); *United States v. Belmont*, 301 U.S. 324 (1937)] do not support the authority that the President asserts in this case. . . .

Medellin argues that the President's Memorandum is a valid exercise of his "Take Care" power. The United States, however, does not rely upon the President's responsibility to "take Care that the Laws be faithfully executed." We think this a wise concession. This authority allows the President to execute the laws, not make them. For the reasons we have stated, the *Avena* judgment is not domestic law; accordingly, the President cannot rely on his Take Care powers here.

☐ *Justice BREYER, with whom Justice SOUTER and Justice GINSBURG join, dissenting.*

The Constitution's Supremacy Clause provides that "all Treaties . . . which shall be made . . . under the Authority of the United States, shall be the supreme Law of the Land; and the Judges in every State shall be bound thereby." The Clause means that the "courts" must regard "a treaty . . . as equivalent to an act of the legislature, whenever it operates of itself without the aid of any legislative provision." *Foster v. Neilson*, 2 Pet. 253 (1829).

In the *Avena* case the International Court of Justice (ICJ) (interpreting and applying the Vienna Convention on Consular Relations) issued a judgment that requires the United States to reexamine certain criminal proceedings in the cases of 51 Mexican nationals. The question here is whether the ICJ's *Avena* judgment is enforceable now as a matter of domestic law, i.e., whether it "operates of itself without the aid" of any further legislation.

The United States has signed and ratified a series of treaties obliging it to comply with ICJ judgments in cases in which it has given its consent to the exercise of the ICJ's adjudicatory authority. Specifically, the United States has agreed to submit, in this kind of case, to the ICJ's "compulsory jurisdiction" for purposes of "compulsory settlement." And it agreed that the ICJ's judgments would have "binding force . . . between the parties and in respect of [a] particular case." United Nations Charter, Art. 59 (1945). President Bush has determined that domestic courts should enforce this particular ICJ judgment. Memorandum to the Attorney General (Feb. 28, 2005) (hereinafter President's Memorandum). And Congress has done nothing to suggest the contrary. Under these circumstances, I believe the treaty obligations, and hence the judgment, resting as it does upon the consent of the United States to the ICJ's jurisdiction, bind the courts no less than would "an act of the [federal] legislature." *Foster.*

To understand the issue before us, the reader must keep in mind three separate ratified United States treaties and one ICJ judgment against the United States. The first treaty, the Vienna Convention, contains two relevant provisions. The first requires the United States and other signatory nations to inform arrested foreign nationals of their separate Convention-given right to contact their nation's consul. The second says that these rights (of an arrested person) "shall be exercised in conformity with the laws and regulations" of the arresting nation, provided that the "laws and regulations . . . enable full effect to be given to the purposes for which" those "rights . . . are intended."

The second treaty, the Optional Protocol, concerns the "compulsory settlement" of Vienna Convention disputes. It provides that for parties that elect to subscribe to the Protocol, "[d]isputes arising out of the interpretation or application of the [Vienna] Convention" shall be submitted to the "compulsory jurisdiction of the International Court of Justice." It authorizes any party that has consented to the ICJ's jurisdiction (by signing the Optional Protocol) to bring another such party before that Court.

The third treaty, the United Nations Charter, says that every signatory Nation "undertakes to comply with the decision of the International Court of Justice in any case to which it is a party." Art. 94(1). In an annex to the Charter, the Statute of the International Court of Justice states that an ICJ judgment has "binding force . . . between the parties and in respect of that particular case." Art. 59.

The critical question here is whether the Supremacy Clause requires Texas to follow, i.e., to enforce, this ICJ judgment. The Court says "no." And it reaches its negative answer by interpreting the labyrinth of treaty provisions as creating a legal obligation that binds the United States internationally, but which, for Supremacy Clause purposes, is not automatically enforceable as domestic law. In the majority's view, the Optional Protocol simply sends the dispute to the ICJ; the ICJ statute says that the ICJ will subsequently reach a judgment; and the U.N. Charter contains no more than a promise to "'undertak[e] to comply'" with that judgment. Such a promise, the majority says, does not as a domestic law matter (in CHIEF JUSTICE MARSHALL's words) "operat[e] of itself without the aid of any legislative provision." *Foster.* Rather, here (and presumably in any other ICJ judgment rendered pursuant to any of the approximately 70 U.S. treaties in force that contain similar provisions for submitting treaty-based disputes to the ICJ for decisions that bind the parties) Congress must enact specific legislation before ICJ judgments entered pursuant to our consent to compulsory ICJ jurisdiction can become domestic law.

In my view, the President has correctly determined that Congress need not enact additional legislation. The majority places too much weight upon treaty language that says little about the matter. The words "undertak[e] to comply," for example, do not tell us whether an ICJ judgment rendered pursuant to the parties' consent to compulsory ICJ jurisdiction does, or does not, automatically become part of our domestic law. To answer that question we must look instead to our own domestic law, in particular, to the many treaty-related cases interpreting the Supremacy Clause. Those cases, including some written by Justices well aware of the Founders' original intent, lead to the conclusion that the ICJ judgment before us is enforceable as a matter of domestic law without further legislation.

Supreme Court case law stretching back more than 200 years helps explain what, for present purposes, the Founders meant when they wrote that "all Treaties . . . shall be the supreme Law of the Land." Art. VI, cl. 2. . . .

Of particular relevance to the present case, the Court has held that the United States may be obligated by treaty to comply with the judgment of an international tribunal interpreting that treaty, despite the absence of any congressional enactment specifically requiring such compliance. See *Comegys v. Vasse*, 1 Pet. 193 (1828) (holding that decision of tribunal rendered pursuant to a United States-Spain treaty, which obliged the parties to "undertake to make satisfaction" of treaty-based rights, was "conclusive and final" and "not re-examinable" in American courts).

All of these cases make clear that self-executing treaty provisions are not uncommon or peculiar creatures of our domestic law; that they cover a wide range of subjects; that the Supremacy Clause itself answers the self-execution question by applying many, but not all, treaty provisions directly to the States;

and that the Clause answers the self-execution question differently than does the law in many other nations. . . .

I would find the relevant treaty provisions self-executing as applied to the ICJ judgment before us (giving that judgment domestic legal effect) for the following reasons, taken together.

First, the language of the relevant treaties strongly supports direct judicial enforceability, at least of judgments of the kind at issue here. The Optional Protocol bears the title "Compulsory Settlement of Disputes," thereby emphasizing the mandatory and binding nature of the procedures it sets forth. The body of the Protocol says specifically that "any party" that has consented to the ICJ's "compulsory jurisdiction" may bring a "dispute" before the court against any other such party. And the Protocol contrasts proceedings of the compulsory kind with an alternative "conciliation procedure," the recommendations of which a party may decide "not" to "accep[t]." Art. III. Thus, the Optional Protocol's basic objective is not just to provide a forum for settlement but to provide a forum for compulsory settlement.

Moreover, in accepting Article 94(1) of the Charter, "[e]ach Member . . . undertakes to comply with the decision" of the ICJ "in any case to which it is a party." And the ICJ Statute (part of the U.N. Charter) makes clear that, a decision of the ICJ between parties that have consented to the ICJ's compulsory jurisdiction has "binding force . . . between the parties and in respect of that particular case.". . .

I recognize, as the majority emphasizes, that the U.N. Charter uses the words "undertakes to comply," rather than, say, "shall comply" or "must comply." But what is inadequate about the word "undertak[e]"? A leading contemporary dictionary defined it in terms of "lay[ing] oneself under obligation . . . to perform or to execute." *Webster's New International Dictionary* (2d ed. 1939). . . .

And even if I agreed with [concurring] Justice STEVENS that the language is perfectly ambiguous (which I do not), I could not agree that "the best reading . . . is . . . one that contemplates future action by the political branches." The consequence of such a reading is to place the fate of an international promise made by the United States in the hands of a single State. And that is precisely the situation that the Framers sought to prevent by enacting the Supremacy Clause. . . .

The upshot is that treaty language says that an ICJ decision is legally binding, but it leaves the implementation of that binding legal obligation to the domestic law of each signatory nation. In this Nation, the Supremacy Clause, as long and consistently interpreted, indicates that ICJ decisions rendered pursuant to provisions for binding adjudication must be domestically legally binding and enforceable in domestic courts at least sometimes. And for purposes of this argument, that conclusion is all that I need. The remainder of the discussion will explain why, if ICJ judgments sometimes bind domestic courts, then they have that effect here.

Second, the Optional Protocol here applies to a dispute about the meaning of a Vienna Convention provision that is itself self-executing and judicially enforceable. The Convention provision is about an individual's "rights," namely, his right upon being arrested to be informed of his separate right to contact his nation's consul. . . .

Third, logic suggests that a treaty provision providing for "final" and "binding" judgments that "settl[e]" treaty-based disputes is self-executing insofar as the judgment in question concerns the meaning of an underlying treaty provision that is itself self-executing. Imagine that two parties to a contract agree to binding arbitration about whether a contract provision's word "grain" includes rye. They would expect that, if the arbitrator decides that the word "grain" does include rye, the arbitrator will then simply read the relevant provision as if it said "grain including rye." They would also expect the arbitrator to issue a binding award that embodies whatever relief would be appropriate under that circumstance.

Why treat differently the parties' agreement to binding ICJ determination about, e.g., the proper interpretation of the Vienna Convention clauses containing the rights here at issue? Why not simply read the relevant Vienna Convention provisions as if (between the parties and in respect to the 51 individuals at issue) they contain words that encapsulate the ICJ's decision? Why would the ICJ judgment not bind in precisely the same way those words would bind if they appeared in the relevant Vienna Convention provisions— just as the ICJ says, for purposes of this case, that they do?

To put the same point differently: What sense would it make (1) to make a self-executing promise and (2) to promise to accept as final an ICJ judgment interpreting that self-executing promise, yet (3) to insist that the judgment itself is not self-executing (i.e., that Congress must enact specific legislation to enforce it)?

I am not aware of any satisfactory answer to these questions. . . .

Fourth, the majority's very different approach has seriously negative practical implications. The United States has entered into at least 70 treaties that contain provisions for ICJ dispute settlement similar to the Protocol before us. Many of these treaties contain provisions similar to those this Court has previously found self-executing—provisions that involve, for example, property rights, contract and commercial rights, trademarks, civil liability for personal injury, rights of foreign diplomats, taxation, domestic-court jurisdiction, and so forth. If the Optional Protocol here, taken together with the U.N. Charter and its annexed ICJ Statute, is insufficient to warrant enforcement of the ICJ judgment before us, it is difficult to see how one could reach a different conclusion in any of these other instances. And the consequence is to undermine longstanding efforts in those treaties to create an effective international system for interpreting and applying many, often commercial, self-executing treaty provisions. . . .

Fifth, other factors, related to the particular judgment here at issue, make that judgment well suited to direct judicial enforcement. The specific issue before the ICJ concerned "'review and reconsideration'" of the "possible prejudice" caused in each of the 51 affected cases by an arresting State's failure to provide the defendant with rights guaranteed by the Vienna Convention. This review will call for an understanding of how criminal procedure works, including whether, and how, a notification failure may work prejudice. As the ICJ itself recognized, "it is the judicial process that is suited to this task." Courts frequently work with criminal procedure and related prejudice. Legislatures do not. Judicial standards are readily available for working in this technical area. Legislative standards are not readily available. Judges typically determine such matters, deciding, for example, whether further hearings are necessary, after reviewing a record in an individual case. Congress does not normally legislate in respect to individual cases. Indeed, to repeat what I said above, what kind of special legislation does the majority believe Congress ought to consider?

Sixth, to find the United States' treaty obligations self-executing as applied to the ICJ judgment (and consequently to find that judgment enforceable) does not threaten constitutional conflict with other branches; it does not require us to engage in nonjudicial activity; and it does not require us to create a new cause of action. The only question before us concerns the application of the ICJ judgment as binding law applicable to the parties in a particular criminal proceeding that Texas law creates independently of the treaty. I repeat that the question before us does not involve the creation of a private right of action (and the majority's reliance on authority regarding such a circumstance is misplaced).

Seventh, neither the President nor Congress has expressed concern about direct judicial enforcement of the ICJ decision. To the contrary, the President favors enforcement of this judgment. . . .

For these seven reasons, I would find that the United States' treaty obligation to comply with the ICJ judgment in *Avena* is enforceable in court in this case without further congressional action beyond Senate ratification of the relevant treaties. The majority reaches a different conclusion because it looks for the wrong thing (explicit textual expression about self-execution) using the wrong standard (clarity) in the wrong place (the treaty language). Hunting for what the text cannot contain, it takes a wrong turn. It threatens to deprive individuals, including businesses, property owners, testamentary beneficiaries, consular officials, and others, of the workable dispute resolution procedures that many treaties, including commercially oriented treaties, provide. In a world where commerce, trade, and travel have become ever more international, that is a step in the wrong direction. . . .

In sum, a strong line of precedent, likely reflecting the views of the Founders, indicates that the treaty provisions before us and the judgment of the International Court of Justice address themselves to the Judicial Branch and consequently are self-executing. In reaching a contrary conclusion, the Court has failed to take proper account of that precedent and, as a result, the Nation may well break its word even though the President seeks to live up to that word and Congress has done nothing to suggest the contrary.

For the reasons set forth, I respectfully dissent.

D | *War-Making and Emergency Powers*

In another rebuke to the Bush administration's position on holding "enemy combatants" without judicial review, a bare majority held that even foreign nationals detained in Guantanamo Bay have the constitutional right to apply to federal courts for writs of *habeas corpus* to review the basis for their detention. Writing for the Court, in *Boumediene v. Bush* (2008) (excerpted below), Justice Kennedy observed, "The laws and Constitution are designed to survive, and remain in force, in extraordinary times." Justice Souter, joined by Justices Ginsburg and Breyer, filed a concurring opinion, while Chief Justice Roberts and Justice Scalia each filed dissenting opinions, which were joined by Justices Thomas and Alito.

In a related case, *Munaf v. Geren*, 128 S.Ct. 2207 (2008), handed down on the same day, a unanimous Court held that U.S. citizens held by U.S. forces in Iraq have the right to file *habeas corpus* petitions, but that federal courts do not have the authority to bar their transfer and trial by Iraqi authorities for charges of terrorism-related crimes. Chief Justice Roberts delivered the opinion of the Court, while Justice Souter filed a concurring opinion, joined by Justices Ginsburg and Breyer. In their view, the ruling would not foreclose U.S. courts from preventing the transfer of citizens into foreign custody when "the probability of torture is well documented, even if the Executive fails to acknowledge it."

■ THE DEVELOPMENT OF LAW

The Treatment of "Enemy Combatants"

Following the Court's ruling in *Boumediene v. Bush* (2008) (excerpted in this chapter), which held that foreign nationals detained in Guantanamo Bay, Cuba, have a constitutional right to apply to federal courts for writs of *habeas corpus* to review their detentions, and which struck down a section of the Military Commissions Act (MCA) of 2006 that eliminated federal court jurisdiction over appeals from detainees, Boumediene was released and transferred to France. The MCA was enacted after the Court's decision in *Hamdan v. Rumsfeld* (2006) (excerpted in Vol. 1, Ch. 3), holding that the Detainee Treatment Act of 2005, which also aimed at stripping federal courts of jurisdiction over detainees' appeals, did not apply to Salim Ahmed Hamdan and others whose appeals were pending at the time of the passage of the law. Subsequently, after the Court's decision, in 2008 Hamdan was transferred to Yemen to serve out his military commission sentence and then released.

In the aftermath of the ruling in *Boumediene*, federal courts in New York and Virginia began reviewing other appeals of detainees, leading to conflicting rulings, while a task force appointed by Democratic President Barak Obama reviewed the status of about 240 "enemy combatants" still held in Guantanamo Bay to decide who to repatriate, try in civilian courts or by military commissions, continue to hold, or transfer to prisons in the United States. In a number of cases, the government reached plea agreements with detainees. In the case of Ali Saleh Kahlah al-Marri, an alleged "sleeper agent" of al Qaeda who was held in a naval brig, the Bush administration asserted the power to indefinitely detain "enemy combatants." The Court of Appeals for the Fourth Circuit upheld the Bush administration and al-Marri appealed to the Supreme Court. But after granting review the Court vacated the lower court's decision, in *Al-Marri v. Spagone*, 129 S.Ct. 1545 (2009), and dismissed the case as moot because the Obama administration decided to indict him on conspiracy charges in federal court.

President Obama campaigned in part on closing Guantanamo Bay and ending the Bush administration's trials of detainees by military commissions. Shortly after coming into the White House, he vowed to eliminate the term "enemy combatants," appointed a task force with the aim of closing Guatanamo Bay by January 2010, defined "waterboarding" as torture, and said he would discontinue trials by military commissions. However, in 2009 he announced that the administration would retain military commissions to try some detainees, while moving others to civilian courts or repatriating them. In doing so, President Obama also promised on May 15, 2009, to reform the military process in five ways: "First, statements that have been obtained from detainees using cruel, inhuman and degrading interrogation methods will no longer be admitted as evidence at trial. Second, the use of hearsay will be limited, so that the burden will no longer be on the party who objects to hearsay to disprove its reliability. Third, the accused will have greater latitude in selecting their counsel. Fourth, basic protections will be provided for those who refuse to testify. And, fifth, military commission judges may establish the jurisdiction of their own courts." Subsequently, President Obama explained that some of the then remaining 240 detainees would be transferred to prisons and tried, some might be returned to their countries of national origin, but some might still be held indefinitely without trials—what he termed "prolonged detention" of those deemed to pose national security risks.

Boumediene v. Bush
128 S.Ct. 2229 (2008)

In 2002, Lakhdar Boumediene and several other Algerian nationals were seized by Bosnian police when U.S. intelligence officers suspected them of plotting to attack an embassy. Boumediene and the others were classified as "enemy combatants" and held in the Naval Base in Guantanamo Bay, Cuba. Boumediene filed a petition for *habeas corpus*, claiming violation of due process and various statutes and treaties. A federal district court granted the government's motion to have all claims dismissed on the ground that Boumediene was an alien detained overseas and, hence, had no right to a *habeas* petition. The U.S. Court of Appeals for the District of Columbia Circuit affirmed, but the U.S. Supreme Court reversed in *Rasul v. Bush*, 542 U.S. 466 (2004) (excerpted in Vol. 1 of the casebook), in holding that noncitizen detainees in Guantanamo were entitled to *habeas* relief. In response, Congress passed the Detainee Treatment Act of 2005, which basically stripped the federal courts of jurisdiction over *habeas* petitions from those held in Guantanamo Bay. The detainees, however, argued that the act did not apply to their cases since they were pending before its passage and that they were denied due process. On appeal, the Supreme Court agreed in *Hamdan v. Rumsfeld*, 548 U.S. 557 (2006) (excerpted in Vol. I of the casebook). Congress in turn passed the Military Commissions Act (MCA) of 2006, which eliminated federal courts' jurisdiction over *habeas* petitions filed by Guantanamo Bay detainees who had been designated "enemy combatants" under the procedures established, after the Court's ruling in *Hamdi v.*

Rumsfeld, 542 U.S. 507 (2004) (excerpted in Vol. 1 of the casebook), for Combatant Status Review Tribunals (CSRTs) to review the military's designation of "enemy combatant" status. Subsequently, Boumediene and other Guantanamo Bay prisoners challenged their detention, but a federal district court agreed with the government and dismissed their petitions. Shortly thereafter, however, another district court rejected the government's motion to dismiss the petitions of other Guantanamo Bay detainees, in ruling that they are entitled to Fifth Amendment due process rights. A divided panel of the U.S. Court of Appeals for the District of Columbia Circuit then vacated the district court judgments and dismissed the cases for lack of jurisdiction. The majority concluded that the Military Commissions Act of 2006 stripped the federal courts of jurisdiction over *habeas* petitions filed by Guantanamo Bay detainees and rejected their claim that the MCA ran afoul of Article 1, Section 9, of the Constitution that stipulates, "The Privilege of the Writ of *Habeas Corpus* shall not be suspended, unless when in Cases of Rebellion or Invasion the public Safety may require it." Boumediene appealed the appellate court's decision and the Supreme Court granted review.

The appellate court's decision was reversed by a bare majority. Justice Kennedy delivered the opinion for the Court. Justice Souter filed a concurring opinion, which Justices Ginsburg and Breyer joined. Chief Justice Roberts and Justice Scalia each filed dissenting opinions, which were joined by Justices Thomas and Alito.

☐ *Justice KENNEDY delivered the opinion of the Court.*

Petitioners present a question not resolved by our earlier cases relating to the detention of aliens at Guantanamo: whether they have the constitutional privilege of *habeas corpus*, a privilege not to be withdrawn except in conformance with the Suspension Clause, Art. I, Sec. 9, cl. 2. We hold these petitioners do have the *habeas corpus* privilege. Congress has enacted a statute, the Detainee Treatment Act of 2005 (DTA), that provides certain procedures for review of the detainees' status. We hold that those procedures are not an adequate and effective substitute for *habeas corpus*. Therefore Sec. 7 of the Military Commissions Act of 2006 (MCA) operates as an unconstitutional suspension of the writ. We do not address whether the President has authority to detain these petitioners nor do we hold that the writ must issue. These and other questions regarding the legality of the detention are to be resolved in the first instance by the District Court.

Under the Authorization for Use of Military Force (AUMF), the President is authorized "to use all necessary and appropriate force against those nations, organizations, or persons he determines planned, authorized, committed, or aided the terrorist attacks that occurred on September 11, 2001, or harbored such organizations or persons, in order to prevent any future acts of international terrorism against the United States by such nations, organizations or persons."

In *Hamdi v. Rumsfeld*, 542 U.S. 507 (2004), five Members of the Court recognized that detention of individuals who fought against the United States in Afghanistan "for the duration of the particular conflict in which they were captured, is so fundamental and accepted an incident to war as to be an exercise of the 'necessary and appropriate force' Congress has authorized the President to use." After *Hamdi*, the Deputy Secretary of Defense established Combatant Status Review Tribunals (CSRTs) to determine whether individuals detained at Guantanamo were "enemy combatants," as the Department defines that term. A later memorandum established procedures to implement the CSRTs. The Government maintains these procedures were designed to comply with the due process requirements identified by the plurality in *Hamdi*....

The first actions commenced in February 2002. The District Court ordered the cases dismissed for lack of jurisdiction because the naval station is outside the sovereign territory of the United States. The Court of Appeals for the District of Columbia Circuit affirmed. We granted *certiorari* and reversed, holding that 28 U.S.C. Sec. 2241 extended statutory *habeas corpus* jurisdiction to Guantanamo. See *Rasul v. Bush*, 542 U.S. 466 (2004). The constitutional issue presented in the instant cases was not reached in *Rasul*.

As a threshold matter, we must decide whether MCA Section 7 denies the federal courts jurisdiction to hear *habeas corpus* actions pending at the time of its enactment. We hold the statute does deny that jurisdiction, so that, if the statute is valid, petitioners' cases must be dismissed....

We acknowledge, moreover, the litigation history that prompted Congress to enact the MCA. In *Hamdan* the Court found it unnecessary to address the petitioner's Suspension Clause arguments but noted the relevance of the clear statement rule in deciding whether Congress intended to reach pending *habeas corpus* cases. This interpretive rule facilitates a dialogue between Congress and the Court. If the Court invokes a clear statement rule to advise that certain statutory interpretations are favored in order to avoid constitutional difficulties, Congress can make an informed legislative choice either to amend the statute or to retain its existing text. If Congress amends, its intent must be respected even if a difficult constitutional question is presented. The usual presumption is that Members of Congress, in accord with their oath of office, considered the constitutional issue and determined the amended statute to be a lawful one; and the Judiciary, in light of that determination, proceeds to its own independent judgment on the constitutional question when required to do so in a proper case.

If this ongoing dialogue between and among the branches of Government is to be respected, we cannot ignore that the MCA was a direct response to *Hamdan*'s holding that the DTA's jurisdiction-stripping provision had no application to pending cases.

In deciding the constitutional questions now presented we must determine whether petitioners are barred from seeking the writ or invoking the protections of the Suspension Clause either because of their status, i.e., petitioners' designation by the Executive Branch as enemy combatants, or their physical location, i.e., their presence at Guantanamo Bay. The Government contends that noncitizens designated as enemy combatants and detained in territory located outside our Nation's borders have no constitutional rights and no privilege of *habeas corpus*. Petitioners contend they do have cognizable constitutional rights and that Congress, in seeking to eliminate recourse to *habeas corpus* as a means to assert those rights, acted in violation of the Suspension Clause.

We begin with a brief account of the history and origins of the writ. Our account proceeds from two propositions. First, protection for the privilege of *habeas corpus* was one of the few safeguards of liberty specified in a Constitution that, at the outset, had no Bill of Rights. In the system conceived by the Framers the writ had a centrality that must inform proper interpretation of the Suspension Clause. Second, to the extent there were settled precedents or legal commentaries in 1789 regarding the extraterritorial scope of the writ or its application to enemy aliens, those authorities can be instructive for the present cases.

The Framers viewed freedom from unlawful restraint as a fundamental precept of liberty, and they understood the writ of *habeas corpus* as a vital instrument to secure that freedom. Experience taught, however, that the common-law writ all too often had been insufficient to guard against the abuse of monarchial power. That history counseled the necessity for specific language in the Constitution to secure the writ and ensure its place in our legal system.

Magna Carta decreed that no man would be imprisoned contrary to the law of the land.

The development was painstaking, even by the centuries-long measures of English constitutional history. The writ was known and used in some form at least as early as the reign of Edward I. Yet at the outset it was used to protect not the rights of citizens but those of the King and his courts. The early courts were considered agents of the Crown, designed to assist the King in the exercise of his power. Thus the writ, while it would become part of the foundation of liberty for the King's subjects, was in its earliest use a mechanism for securing compliance with the King's laws. . . .

Still, the writ proved to be an imperfect check. Even when the importance of the writ was well understood in England, *habeas* relief often was denied by the courts or suspended by Parliament. Denial or suspension occurred in times of political unrest, to the anguish of the imprisoned and the outrage of those in sympathy with them. . . .

This history was known to the Framers. It no doubt confirmed their view that pendular swings to and away from individual liberty were endemic to undivided, uncontrolled power. The Framers' inherent distrust of governmental power was the driving force behind the constitutional plan that allocated powers among three independent branches. This design serves not only to make Government accountable but also to secure individual liberty. . . .

That the Framers considered the writ a vital instrument for the protection of individual liberty is evident from the care taken to specify the limited grounds for its suspension: "The Privilege of the Writ of *Habeas Corpus* shall not be suspended, unless when in Cases of Rebellion or Invasion the public Safety may require it." Art. I, Sec. 9, cl. 2. The word "privilege" was used, perhaps, to avoid mentioning some rights to the exclusion of others. (Indeed, the only mention of the term "right" in the Constitution, as ratified, is in its clause giving Congress the power to protect the rights of authors and inventors. See Art. I, Sec. 8, cl. 8.)

Surviving accounts of the ratification debates provide additional evidence that the Framers deemed the writ to be an essential mechanism in the separation-of-powers scheme. . . .

Post-1789 *habeas* developments in England, though not bearing upon the Framers' intent, do verify their foresight. Those later events would underscore the need for structural barriers against arbitrary suspensions of the writ. Just as the writ had been vulnerable to executive and parliamentary encroachment on both sides of the Atlantic before the American Revolution, despite the *Habeas Corpus* Act of 1679, the writ was suspended with frequency in England during times of political unrest after 1789. Parliament suspended the writ for much of the period from 1792 to 1801, resulting in rampant arbitrary imprisonment.

In our own system the Suspension Clause is designed to protect against these cyclical abuses. The Clause protects the rights of the detained by a means consistent with the essential design of the Constitution. It ensures that, except during periods of formal suspension, the Judiciary will have a time-tested device, the writ, to maintain the "delicate balance of governance" that is itself the surest safeguard of liberty. The Clause protects the rights of the detained by affirming the duty and authority of the Judiciary to call the jailer to account. The separation-of-powers doctrine, and the history that influenced its design, therefore must inform the reach and purpose of the Suspension Clause.

The broad historical narrative of the writ and its function is central to our analysis, but we seek guidance as well from founding-era authorities addressing the specific question before us: whether foreign nationals, apprehended and detained in distant countries during a time of serious threats to our Nation's security, may assert the privilege of the writ and seek its protection. The Court has been careful not to foreclose the possibility that the protections of the Suspension Clause have expanded along with post-1789 developments that define the present scope of the writ. . . .

We know that at common law a petitioner's status as an alien was not a categorical bar to *habeas corpus* relief. See, e.g., *Sommersett's Case*, 20 How. St. Tr. 1 (1772) (ordering an African slave freed upon finding the custodian's return insufficient). . . .

We find the evidence as to the geographic scope of the writ at common law informative, but, again, not dispositive. Petitioners argue the site of their detention is analogous to two territories outside of England to which the writ did run: the so-called "exempt jurisdictions," like the Channel Islands; and (in former times) India. There are critical differences between these places and Guantanamo, however.

As the Court noted in *Rasul*, common-law courts granted *habeas corpus* relief to prisoners detained in the exempt jurisdictions. But these areas, while not in theory part of the realm of England, were nonetheless under the Crown's control. And there is some indication that these jurisdictions were considered sovereign territory. Because the United States does not maintain formal sovereignty over Guantanamo Bay, the naval station there and the exempt jurisdictions discussed in the English authorities are not similarly situated. . . .

In the end a categorical or formal conception of sovereignty does not provide a comprehensive or altogether satisfactory explanation for the general understanding that prevailed when Lord Mansfield considered issuance of the writ outside England. In 1759 the writ did not run to Scotland but did run to Ireland, even though, at that point, Scotland and England had merged under the rule of a single sovereign, whereas the Crowns of Great Britain and Ireland remained separate (at least in theory). But there was at least one major difference between Scotland's and Ireland's relationship with England during this period that might explain why the writ ran to Ireland but not to Scotland. English law did not generally apply in Scotland (even after the Act of Union) but it did apply in Ireland. . . .

The prudential barriers that may have prevented the English courts from issuing the writ to Scotland and Hanover are not relevant here. We have no reason to believe an order from a federal court would be disobeyed at Guantanamo. No Cuban court has jurisdiction to hear these petitioners' claims, and no law other than the laws of the United States applies at the naval station. The modern-day relations between the United States and Guantanamo thus differ in important respects from the 18th-century relations between

England and the kingdoms of Scotland and Hanover. This is reason enough for us to discount the relevance of the Government's analogy. . . .

Drawing from its position that at common law the writ ran only to territories over which the Crown was sovereign, the Government says the Suspension Clause affords petitioners no rights because the United States does not claim sovereignty over the place of detention.

Guantanamo Bay is not formally part of the United States. And under the terms of the lease between the United States and Cuba, Cuba retains "ultimate sovereignty" over the territory while the United States exercises "complete jurisdiction and control." Under the terms of the 1934 Treaty, however, Cuba effectively has no rights as a sovereign until the parties agree to modification of the 1903 Lease Agreement or the United States abandons the base. . . .

Were we to hold that the present cases turn on the political question doctrine, we would be required first to accept the Government's premise that *de jure* sovereignty is the touchstone of *habeas corpus* jurisdiction. This premise, however, is unfounded. For the reasons indicated above, the history of common-law *habeas corpus* provides scant support for this proposition; and, for the reasons indicated below, that position would be inconsistent with our precedents and contrary to fundamental separation-of-powers principles.

The Court has discussed the issue of the Constitution's extraterritorial application on many occasions. These decisions undermine the Government's argument that, at least as applied to noncitizens, the Constitution necessarily stops where *de jure* sovereignty ends. . . .

Fundamental questions regarding the Constitution's geographic scope first arose at the dawn of the 20th century when the Nation acquired noncontiguous Territories: Puerto Rico, Guam, and the Philippines—ceded to the United States by Spain at the conclusion of the Spanish-American War—and Hawaii—annexed by the United States in 1898. At this point Congress chose to discontinue its previous practice of extending constitutional rights to the territories by statute.

In a series of opinions later known as the *Insular Cases*, the Court addressed whether the Constitution, by its own force, applies in any territory that is not a State. The Court held that the Constitution has independent force in these territories, a force not contingent upon acts of legislative grace. Yet it took note of the difficulties inherent in that position.

Prior to their cession to the United States, the former Spanish colonies operated under a civil-law system, without experience in the various aspects of the Anglo-American legal tradition, for instance the use of grand and petit juries. At least with regard to the Philippines, a complete transformation of the prevailing legal culture would have been not only disruptive but also unnecessary, as the United States intended to grant independence to that Territory. The Court thus was reluctant to risk the uncertainty and instability that could result from a rule that displaced altogether the existing legal systems in these newly acquired Territories.

These considerations resulted in the doctrine of territorial incorporation, under which the Constitution applies in full in incorporated Territories surely destined for statehood but only in part in unincorporated Territories. . . .

Practical considerations weighed heavily as well in *Johnson v. Eisentrager*, 339 U.S. 763 (1950), where the Court addressed whether *habeas corpus* jurisdiction extended to enemy aliens who had been convicted of violating the laws of war. The prisoners were detained at Landsberg Prison in Germany during the Allied Powers' postwar occupation. The Court stressed the difficulties of ordering the Government to produce the prisoners in a *habeas corpus* proceeding. It "would require allocation of shipping space, guarding personnel, billeting and rations" and would damage the prestige of military commanders at a sensitive time. In considering these factors the Court sought to balance the constraints of military occupation with constitutional necessities.

True, the Court in *Eisentrager* denied access to the writ, and it noted the prisoners "at no relevant time were within any territory over which the United States is sovereign, and [that] the scenes of their offense, their capture, their trial and their punishment were all beyond the territorial jurisdiction of any court of the United States." The Government seizes upon this language as proof positive that the *Eisentrager* Court adopted a formalistic, sovereignty-based test for determining the reach of the Suspension Clause. We reject this reading for three reasons.

First, we do not accept the idea that the above-quoted passage from *Eisentrager* is the only authoritative language in the opinion and that all the rest is *dicta*.

Second, because the United States lacked both *de jure* sovereignty and plenary control over Landsberg Prison, it is far from clear that the *Eisentrager* Court used the term sovereignty only in the narrow technical sense and not to connote the degree of control the military asserted over the facility. . . .

Third, if the Government's reading of *Eisentrager* were correct, the opinion would have marked not only a change in, but a complete repudiation of, the *Insular Cases'* functional approach to questions of extraterritoriality. We cannot accept the Government's view. Nothing in *Eisentrager* says that *de jure* sovereignty is or has ever been the only relevant consideration in determining the geographic reach of the Constitution or of *habeas corpus*. Were that the case, there would be considerable tension between *Eisentrager*, on the one hand, and the *Insular Cases*, on the other. Our cases need not be read to conflict in this manner. A constricted reading of *Eisentrager* overlooks what we see as a common thread uniting the *Insular Cases* [and] *Eisentrager*; the idea that questions of extraterritoriality turn on objective factors and practical concerns, not formalism.

The Government's formal sovereignty-based test raises troubling separation-of-powers concerns as well. The political history of Guantanamo illustrates the deficiencies of this approach. The United States has maintained complete and uninterrupted control of the bay for over 100 years. At the close of the Spanish-American War, Spain ceded control over the entire island of Cuba to the United States and specifically "relinquishe[d] all claim[s] of sovereignty . . . and title." See Treaty of Paris, Dec. 10, 1898. From the date the treaty with Spain was signed until the Cuban Republic was established on May 20, 1902, the United States governed the territory "in trust" for the benefit of the Cuban people. And although it recognized, by entering into the 1903 Lease Agreement, that Cuba retained "ultimate sovereignty" over Guantanamo, the United States continued to maintain the same plenary control it had enjoyed since 1898. . . .

The Constitution grants Congress and the President the power to acquire, dispose of, and govern territory, not the power to decide when and where its terms apply. Even when the United States acts outside its borders, its powers are not "absolute and unlimited" but are subject "to such restrictions as are expressed in the Constitution." *Murphy v. Ramsey*, 114 U.S. 15 (1885). . . .

As we recognized in *Rasul*, the outlines of a framework for determining the reach of the Suspension Clause are suggested by the factors the Court relied upon in *Eisentrager*. In addition to the practical concerns discussed above, the *Eisentrager* Court found relevant that each petitioner: "(a) is an enemy alien; (b) has never been or resided in the United States; (c) was captured outside of our territory and there held in military custody as a prisoner of war; (d) was tried and convicted by a Military Commission sitting outside the United States; (e) for offenses against laws of war committed outside the United States; (f) and is at all times imprisoned outside the United States." Based on this language from *Eisentrager*, and the reasoning in our other extra-territoriality opinions, we conclude that at least three factors are relevant in determining the reach of the Suspension Clause: (1) the citizenship and status of the detainee and the adequacy of the process through which that status determination was made; (2) the nature of the sites where apprehension and then detention took place; and (3) the practical obstacles inherent in resolving the prisoner's entitlement to the writ.

Applying this framework, we note at the onset that the status of these detainees is a matter of dispute. The petitioners, like those in *Eisentrager*, are not American citizens. But the petitioners in *Eisentrager* did not contest, it seems, the Court's assertion that they were "enemy alien[s]." In the instant cases, by contrast, the detainees deny they are enemy combatants. They have been afforded some process in CSRT proceedings to determine their status; but, unlike in *Eisentrager*, there has been no trial by military commission for violations of the laws of war. The difference is not trivial. The records from the *Eisentrager* trials suggest that, well before the petitioners brought their case to this Court, there had been a rigorous adversarial process to test the legality of their detention. The *Eisentrager* petitioners were charged by a bill of particulars that made detailed factual allegations against them. To rebut the accusations, they were entitled to representation by counsel, allowed to introduce evidence on their own behalf, and permitted to cross-examine the prosecution's witnesses.

In comparison the procedural protections afforded to the detainees in the CSRT hearings are far more limited, and, we conclude, fall well short of the procedures and adversarial mechanisms that would eliminate the need for *habeas corpus* review. Although the detainee is assigned a "Personal Representative" to assist him during CSRT proceedings, the Secretary of the Navy's memorandum makes clear that person is not the detainee's lawyer or even his "advocate." The Government's evidence is accorded a presumption of validity. The detainee is allowed to present "reasonably available" evidence, but his ability to rebut the Government's evidence against him is limited by the circumstances of his confinement and his lack of counsel at this stage. And although the detainee can seek review of his status determination in the Court of Appeals, that review process cannot cure all defects in the earlier proceedings.

As to the second factor relevant to this analysis, the detainees here are similarly situated to the *Eisentrager* petitioners in that the sites of their apprehension and detention are technically outside the sovereign territory of the United States. . . .

As to the third factor, we recognize, as the Court did in *Eisentrager*, that there are costs to holding the Suspension Clause applicable in a case of military detention abroad. *Habeas corpus* proceedings may require expenditure of funds by the Government and may divert the attention of military personnel from other pressing tasks. While we are sensitive to these concerns, we do not find them dispositive. Compliance with any judicial process requires some incremental expenditure of resources. Yet civilian courts and the Armed Forces have functioned along side each other at various points in our history. . . .

We hold that Art. I, Sec. 9, cl. 2, of the Constitution has full effect at Guantanamo Bay. If the privilege of *habeas corpus* is to be denied to the detainees now before us, Congress must act in accordance with the requirements of the Suspension Clause. The MCA does not purport to be a formal suspension of the writ; and the Government, in its submissions to us, has not argued that it is. Petitioners, therefore, are entitled to the privilege of *habeas corpus* to challenge the legality of their detention.

In light of this holding the question becomes whether the statute stripping jurisdiction to issue the writ avoids the Suspension Clause mandate because Congress has provided adequate substitute procedures for *habeas corpus*. The Government submits there has been compliance with the Suspension Clause because the DTA review process in the Court of Appeals provides an adequate substitute. Congress has granted that court jurisdiction to consider "(i) whether the status determination of the [CSRT] . . . was consistent with the standards and procedures specified by the Secretary of Defense . . . and (ii) to the extent the Constitution and laws of the United States are applicable, whether the use of such standards and procedures to make the determination is consistent with the Constitution and laws of the United States." . . .

Our case law does not contain extensive discussion of standards defining suspension of the writ or of circumstances under which suspension has occurred. This simply confirms the care Congress has taken throughout our Nation's history to preserve the writ and its function. Indeed, most of the major legislative enactments pertaining to *habeas corpus* have acted not to contract the writ's protection but to expand it or to hasten resolution of prisoners' claims.

We do not endeavor to offer a comprehensive summary of the requisites for an adequate substitute for *habeas corpus*. We do consider it uncontroversial, however, that the privilege of *habeas corpus* entitles the prisoner to a meaningful opportunity to demonstrate that he is being held pursuant to "the erroneous application or interpretation" of relevant law. And the *habeas* court must have the power to order the conditional release of an individual unlawfully detained—though release need not be the exclusive remedy and is not the appropriate one in every case in which the writ is granted. . . .

[W]here relief is sought from a sentence that resulted from the judgment of a court of record, as was the case in *Watkins* and indeed in most federal *habeas* cases, considerable deference is owed to the court that ordered confinement. . . .

Where a person is detained by executive order, rather than, say, after being tried and convicted in a court, the need for collateral review is most pressing. A criminal conviction in the usual course occurs after a judicial hearing before a tribunal disinterested in the outcome and committed to procedures designed to ensure its own independence. These dynamics are not inherent in executive detention orders or executive review procedures. In this context the need for *habeas corpus* is more urgent. The intended duration of the detention and the reasons for it bear upon the precise scope of the inquiry. *Habeas corpus* proceedings need not resemble a criminal trial, even when the detention is by executive order. But the writ must be effective. The *habeas* court must have sufficient authority to conduct a meaningful review of both the cause for detention and the Executive's power to detain.

To determine the necessary scope of *habeas corpus* review, therefore, we must assess the CSRT process, the mechanism through which petitioners' designation as enemy combatants became final. Whether one characterizes the CSRT process as direct review of the Executive's battlefield determination that the detainee is an enemy combatant—as the parties have and as we do—or as the first step in the collateral review of a battlefield determination makes no difference in a proper analysis of whether the procedures Congress put in place are an adequate substitute for *habeas corpus*. What matters is the sum total of procedural protections afforded to the detainee at all stages, direct and collateral. Petitioners identify what they see as myriad deficiencies in the CSRTs. The most relevant for our purposes are the constraints upon the detainee's ability to rebut the factual basis for the Government's assertion that he is an enemy combatant. As already noted, at the CSRT stage the detainee has limited means to find or present evidence to challenge the Government's case against him. He does not have the assistance of counsel and may not be aware of the most critical allegations that the Government relied upon to order his detention. The detainee can confront witnesses that testify during the CSRT proceedings. But given that there are in effect no limits on the admission of hearsay evidence—the only requirement is that the tribunal deem the evidence "relevant and helpful"—the detainee's opportunity to question witnesses is likely to be more theoretical than real. . . .

Even if we were to assume that the CSRTs satisfy due process standards, it would not end our inquiry. *Habeas corpus* is a collateral process that exists, in Justice HOLMES' words, to "cu[t] through all forms and g[o] to the very tissue of the structure. It comes in from the outside, not in subordination to the proceedings, and although every form may have been preserved opens the inquiry whether they have been more than an empty shell." *Frank v. Mangum*, 237 U.S. 309 (1915). Even when the procedures authorizing detention are structurally sound, the Suspension Clause remains applicable and the writ relevant. . . .

Although we make no judgment as to whether the CSRTs, as currently constituted, satisfy due process standards, we agree with petitioners that, even when all the parties involved in this process act with diligence and in good faith, there is considerable risk of error in the tribunal's findings of fact. And given that the consequence of error may be detention of persons for the duration of hostilities that may last a generation or more, this is a risk too significant to ignore.

For the writ of *habeas corpus*, or its substitute, to function as an effective and proper remedy in this context, the court that conducts the *habeas* proceeding must have the means to correct errors that occurred during the CSRT proceedings. This includes some authority to assess the sufficiency of the Government's evidence against the detainee. It also must have the authority to admit and consider relevant exculpatory evidence that was not introduced during the earlier proceeding. Federal *habeas* petitioners long have had the means to supplement the record on review, even in the post conviction *habeas* setting. Here that opportunity is constitutionally required.

Consistent with the historic function and province of the writ, *habeas corpus* review may be more circumscribed if the underlying detention proceedings are more thorough than they were here. In two *habeas* cases involving enemy aliens tried for war crimes, *In re Yamashita*, 327 U.S. 1 (1946), and *Ex parte Quirin*, 317 U.S. 1 (1942), for example, this Court limited its review to determining whether the Executive had legal authority to try the petitioners by military commission. We need not revisit these cases, however. For on their own terms, the proceedings in *Yamashita* and *Quirin*, like those in *Eisentrager*, had an adversarial structure that is lacking here.

The extent of the showing required of the Government in these cases is a matter to be determined. We need not explore it further at this stage. We do hold that when the judicial power to issue *habeas corpus* properly is invoked the judicial officer must have adequate authority to make a determination in light of the relevant law and facts and to formulate and issue appropriate orders for relief, including, if necessary, an order directing the prisoner's release.

We now consider whether the DTA allows the Court of Appeals to conduct a proceeding meeting these standards. . . .

The DTA does not explicitly empower the Court of Appeals to order the applicant in a DTA review proceeding released should the court find that the standards and procedures used at his CSRT hearing were insufficient to justify detention. This is troubling. Yet, for present purposes, we can assume congressional silence permits a constitutionally required remedy. In that case it would be possible to hold that a remedy of release is impliedly provided for. . . .

The absence of a release remedy and specific language allowing AUMF challenges are not the only constitutional infirmities from which the statute potentially suffers, however. The more difficult question is whether the DTA permits the Court of Appeals to make requisite findings of fact. The DTA enables petitioners to request "review" of their CSRT determination in the Court of Appeals, but the "Scope of Review" provision confines the Court of Appeals' role to reviewing whether the CSRT followed the "standards and procedures" issued by the Department of Defense and assessing whether those "standards and procedures" are lawful. Among these standards is "the requirement that the conclusion of the Tribunal be supported by a preponderance of the evidence . . . allowing a rebuttable presumption in favor of the Government's evidence."

Assuming the DTA can be construed to allow the Court of Appeals to review or correct the CSRT's factual determinations, as opposed to merely certifying that the tribunal applied the correct standard of proof, we see no way to construe the statute to allow what is also constitutionally required in this context: an opportunity for the detainee to present relevant exculpatory evidence that was not made part of the record in the earlier proceedings.

On its face the statute allows the Court of Appeals to consider no evidence outside the CSRT record. In the parallel litigation, however, the Court of Appeals determined that the DTA allows it to order the production of all "'reasonably available information in the possession of the U.S. Government bearing on the issue of whether the detainee meets the criteria to be designated as an enemy combatant,'" regardless of whether this evidence was put before the CSRT. For present purposes, we can assume that the Court of Appeals was correct that the DTA allows introduction and consideration of relevant exculpatory evidence that was "reasonably available" to the Government at the time of the CSRT but not made part of the record. Even so, the DTA review proceeding falls short of being a constitutionally adequate substitute, for the detainee still would have no opportunity to present evidence discovered after the CSRT proceedings concluded.

Under the DTA the Court of Appeals has the power to review CSRT determinations by assessing the legality of standards and procedures. This implies the power to inquire into what happened at the CSRT hearing and, perhaps, to remedy certain deficiencies in that proceeding. But should the Court of Appeals determine that the CSRT followed appropriate and lawful standards and procedures, it will have reached the limits of its jurisdiction. There is no language in the DTA that can be construed to allow the Court of Appeals to admit and consider newly discovered evidence that could not have been made part of the CSRT record because it was unavailable to either the Government or the detainee when the CSRT made its findings. This evidence, however, may be critical to the detainee's argument that he is not an enemy combatant and there is no cause to detain him. . . .

By foreclosing consideration of evidence not presented or reasonably available to the detainee at the CSRT proceedings, the DTA disadvantages the detainee by limiting the scope of collateral review to a record that may not be accurate or complete. In other contexts, e.g., in post-trial *habeas* cases where the prisoner already has had a full and fair opportunity to develop the factual predicate of his claims, similar limitations on the scope of *habeas* review may be appropriate. In this context, however, where the underlying detention proceedings lack the necessary adversarial character, the detainee cannot be held responsible for all deficiencies in the record. . . .

We do not imply DTA review would be a constitutionally sufficient replacement for *habeas corpus* but for these limitations on the detainee's ability to present exculpatory evidence. For even if it were possible, as a textual matter, to read into the statute each of the necessary procedures we have identified, we could not overlook the cumulative effect of our doing so. To hold that the detainees at Guantanamo may, under the DTA, challenge the President's legal authority to detain them, contest the CSRT's findings of fact, supplement the record on review with exculpatory evidence, and request an order of release would come close to reinstating the *habeas corpus* process Congress sought to deny them. The language of the statute, read in light of Congress' reasons for enacting it, cannot bear this interpretation. Petitioners have met their burden of establishing that the DTA review process is, on its face, an inadequate substitute for *habeas corpus*. . . .

Although we hold that the DTA is not an adequate and effective substitute for *habeas corpus*, it does not follow that a *habeas corpus* court may disregard the dangers the detention in these cases was intended to prevent. [T]he Suspension Clause does not resist innovation in the field of *habeas corpus*. Certain accommodations can be made to reduce the burden *habeas corpus* proceedings will place on the military without impermissibly diluting the protections of the writ. . . .

In considering both the procedural and substantive standards used to impose detention to prevent acts of terrorism, proper deference must be accorded to the political branches. See *United States v. Curtiss-Wright Export Corp.*, 299 U.S. 304 (1936). Unlike the President and some designated Members of Congress, neither the Members of this Court nor most federal judges begin the day with briefings that may describe new and serious threats to our Nation and its people. The law must accord the Executive substantial authority to apprehend and detain those who pose a real danger to our security. . . .

It bears repeating that our opinion does not address the content of the law that governs petitioners' detention. That is a matter yet to be determined. We hold that petitioners may invoke the fundamental procedural protections of *habeas corpus*. The laws and Constitution are designed to survive, and remain in force, in extraordinary times. Liberty and security can be reconciled; and in our system they are reconciled within the framework of the law. The Framers decided that *habeas corpus*, a right of first importance, must be a part of that framework, a part of that law.

The determination by the Court of Appeals that the Suspension Clause and its protections are inapplicable to petitioners was in error. The judgment of the Court of Appeals is reversed. The cases are remanded to the Court of

Appeals with instructions that it remand the cases to the District Court for proceedings consistent with this opinion. It is so ordered.

☐ *Justice SOUTER, with whom Justice GINSBURG and Justice BREYER join, concurring.*

Four years ago, this Court in *Rasul v. Bush*, 542 U.S. 466 (2004) held that statutory *habeas* jurisdiction extended to claims of foreign nationals imprisoned by the United States at Guantanamo Bay, "to determine the legality of the Executive's potentially indefinite detention" of them. Subsequent legislation eliminated the statutory *habeas* jurisdiction over these claims, so that now there must be constitutionally based jurisdiction or none at all. Justice SCALIA is thus correct that here, for the first time, this Court holds there is (he says "confers") constitutional *habeas* jurisdiction over aliens imprisoned by the military outside an area of *de jure* national sovereignty. But no one who reads the Court's opinion in *Rasul* could seriously doubt that the jurisdictional question must be answered the same way in purely constitutional cases, given the Court's reliance on the historical background of *habeas* generally in answering the statutory question.

Indeed, the Court in *Rasul* directly answered the very historical question that Justice SCALIA says is dispositive; it wrote that "[a]pplication of the *habeas* statute to persons detained at [Guantanamo] is consistent with the historical reach of the writ of *habeas corpus*," Justice SCALIA dismisses the statement as *dictum*, but if *dictum* it was, it was *dictum* well considered, and it stated the view of five Members of this Court on the historical scope of the writ. Of course, it takes more than a quotation from *Rasul*, however much on point, to resolve the constitutional issue before us here, which the majority opinion has explored afresh in the detail it deserves. But whether one agrees or disagrees with today's decision, it is no bolt out of the blue.

A second fact insufficiently appreciated by the dissents is the length of the disputed imprisonments, some of the prisoners represented here today having been locked up for six years. Hence the hollow ring when the dissenters suggest that the Court is somehow precipitating the judiciary into reviewing claims that the military (subject to appeal to the Court of Appeals for the District of Columbia Circuit) could handle within some reasonable period of time. . . .

It is in fact the very lapse of four years from the time *Rasul* put everyone on notice that *habeas* process was available to Guantanamo prisoners, and the lapse of six years since some of these prisoners were captured and incarcerated, that stand at odds with the repeated suggestions of the dissenters that these cases should be seen as a judicial victory in a contest for power between the Court and the political branches. The several answers to the charge of triumphalism might start with a basic fact of Anglo-American constitutional history: that the power, first of the Crown and now of the Executive Branch of the United States, is necessarily limited by *habeas corpus* jurisdiction to enquire into the legality of executive detention. And one could explain that in this Court's exercise of responsibility to preserve *habeas corpus* something much more significant is involved than pulling and hauling between the judicial and political branches. Instead, though, it is enough to repeat that some of these petitioners have spent six years behind bars. After six years of sustained executive detentions in Guantanamo, subject to *habeas* jurisdiction but without any actual *habeas* scrutiny, today's decision is no judicial victory, but an act of perseverance in trying to make *habeas* review, and the obligation of the courts to provide it, mean something of value both to prisoners and to the Nation.

☐ *Justice SCALIA, with whom THE CHIEF JUSTICE, Justice THOMAS, and Justice ALITO join, dissenting.*

Today, for the first time in our Nation's history, the Court confers a constitutional right to *habeas corpus* on alien enemies detained abroad by our military forces in the course of an ongoing war. The CHIEF JUSTICE's dissent, which I join, shows that the procedures prescribed by Congress in the Detainee Treatment Act provide the essential protections that *habeas corpus* guarantees; there has thus been no suspension of the writ, and no basis exists for judicial intervention beyond what the Act allows. My problem with today's opinion is more fundamental still: The writ of *habeas corpus* does not, and never has, run in favor of aliens abroad; the Suspension Clause thus has no application, and the Court's intervention in this military matter is entirely *ultra vires*.

I shall devote most of what will be a lengthy opinion to the legal errors contained in the opinion of the Court. Contrary to my usual practice, however, I think it appropriate to begin with a description of the disastrous consequences of what the Court has done today.

America is at war with radical Islamists. The enemy began by killing Americans and American allies abroad: 241 at the Marine barracks in Lebanon, 19 at the Khobar Towers in Dhahran, 224 at our embassies in Dar es Salaam and Nairobi, and 17 on the USS Cole in Yemen. On September 11, 2001, the enemy brought the battle to American soil, killing 2,749 at the Twin Towers in New York City, 184 at the Pentagon in Washington, D. C., and 40 in Pennsylvania. It has threatened further attacks against our homeland; one need only walk about buttressed and barricaded Washington, or board a plane anywhere in the country, to know that the threat is a serious one. Our Armed Forces are now in the field against the enemy, in Afghanistan and Iraq.

The game of bait-and-switch that today's opinion plays upon the Nation's Commander in Chief will make the war harder on us. It will almost certainly cause more Americans to be killed. That consequence would be tolerable if necessary to preserve a time-honored legal principle vital to our constitutional Republic. But it is this Court's blatant abandonment of such a principle that produces the decision today. . . .

In the long term, then, the Court's decision today accomplishes little, except perhaps to reduce the well-being of enemy combatants that the Court ostensibly seeks to protect. In the short term, however, the decision is devastating. At least 30 of those prisoners hitherto released from Guantanamo Bay have returned to the battlefield. But others have succeeded in carrying on their atrocities against innocent civilians. In one case, a detainee released from Guantanamo Bay masterminded the kidnapping of two Chinese dam workers, one of whom was later shot to death when used as a human shield against Pakistani commandoes.

These, mind you, were detainees whom the military had concluded were not enemy combatants. Their return to the kill illustrates the incredible difficulty of assessing who is and who is not an enemy combatant in a foreign theater of operations where the environment does not lend itself to rigorous evidence collection. Astoundingly, the Court today raises the bar, requiring military officials to appear before civilian courts and defend their decisions under procedural and evidentiary rules that go beyond what Congress has specified. . . .

And today it is not just the military that the Court elbows aside. A mere two Terms ago in *Hamdan v. Rumsfeld*, 548 U.S. 557 (2006), when the Court held (quite amazingly) that the Detainee Treatment Act of 2005 had not stripped *habeas* jurisdiction over Guantanamo petitioners' claims, four Members of today's five-Justice majority joined an opinion saying the following: "Nothing prevents the President from returning to Congress to seek the authority [for trial by military commission] he believes necessary." . . .

The Suspension Clause of the Constitution provides: "The Privilege of the Writ of *Habeas Corpus* shall not be suspended, unless when in Cases of Rebellion or Invasion the public Safety may require it." Art. I, Sec. 9, cl. 2. As a court of law operating under a written Constitution, our role is to determine whether there is a conflict between that Clause and the Military Commissions Act. A conflict arises only if the Suspension Clause preserves the privilege of the writ for aliens held by the United States military as enemy combatants at the base in Guantanamo Bay, located within the sovereign territory of Cuba.

We have frequently stated that we owe great deference to Congress's view that a law it has passed is constitutional. Indeed, we accord great deference even when the President acts alone in this area.

In light of those principles of deference, the Court's conclusion that "the common law [does not] yiel[d] a definite answer to the questions before us," leaves it no choice but to affirm the Court of Appeals. The writ as preserved in the Constitution could not possibly extend farther than the common law provided when that Clause was written. The Court admits that it cannot determine whether the writ historically extended to aliens held abroad, and it concedes (necessarily) that Guantanamo Bay lies outside the sovereign territory of the United States. Together, these two concessions establish that it is (in the Court's view) perfectly ambiguous whether the common-law writ would have provided a remedy for these petitioners. If that is so, the Court has no basis to strike down the Military Commissions Act, and must leave undisturbed the considered judgment of the coequal branches.

How, then, does the Court weave a clear constitutional prohibition out of pure interpretive equipoise? The Court resorts to "fundamental separation-of-powers principles" to interpret the Suspension Clause. According to the Court, because "the writ of *habeas corpus* is itself an indispensable mechanism for monitoring the separation of powers," the test of its extraterritorial reach "must not be subject to manipulation by those whose power it is designed to restrain."

That approach distorts the nature of the separation of powers and its role in the constitutional structure. The "fundamental separation-of-powers principles" that the Constitution embodies are to be derived not from some judicially imagined matrix, but from the sum total of the individual separation-of-powers provisions that the Constitution sets forth. Only by considering them one-by-one does the full shape of the Constitution's separation-of-powers principles emerge. It is nonsensical to interpret those provisions themselves in light of some general "separation-of-powers principles" dreamed up by the Court. Rather, they must be interpreted to mean what they were understood to mean when the people ratified them. And if the understood scope of the writ of *habeas corpus* was "designed to restrain" (as the Court says) the actions of the Executive, the understood limits upon that scope were (as the Court seems not to grasp) just as much "designed to restrain" the incursions of the Third Branch. "Manipulation" of the territorial reach of the writ by the Judiciary poses just as much a threat to the proper separation of powers as "manipulation" by the Executive. . . .

The Court purports to derive from our precedents a "functional" test for the extraterritorial reach of the writ, which shows that the Military Commissions Act unconstitutionally restricts the scope of *habeas*. That is remarkable because the most pertinent of those precedents, *Johnson v. Eisentrager*, conclusively establishes the opposite. There we were confronted with the claims of 21 Germans held at Landsberg Prison, an American military facility located in the American Zone of occupation in postwar Germany. They had been captured in China, and an American military commission sitting there had convicted them of war crimes—collaborating with the Japanese after Germany's surrender. Like the petitioners here, the Germans claimed that their detentions violated the Constitution and international law, and sought a writ of *habeas corpus*. Writing for the Court, Justice JACKSON held that American courts lacked *habeas* jurisdiction: "We are cited to [sic] no instance where a court, in this or any other country where the writ is known, has issued it on behalf of an alien enemy who, at no relevant time and in no stage of his captivity, has been within its territorial jurisdiction. Nothing in the text of the Constitution extends such a right, nor does anything in our statutes." Justice JACKSON then elaborated on the historical scope of the writ: "The alien, to whom the United States has been traditionally hospitable, has been accorded a generous and ascending scale of rights as he increases his identity with our society." "But, in extending constitutional protections beyond the citizenry, the Court has been at pains to point out that it was the alien's presence within its territorial jurisdiction that gave the Judiciary power to act." . . .

Eisentrager thus held—held beyond any doubt—that the Constitution does not ensure habeas for aliens held by the United States in areas over which our Government is not sovereign.

The Court would have us believe that *Eisentrager* rested on "[p]ractical considerations," such as the "difficulties of ordering the Government to produce the prisoners in a *habeas corpus* proceeding." Formal sovereignty, says the Court, is merely one consideration "that bears upon which constitutional guarantees apply" in a given location. This is a sheer rewriting of the case. *Eisentrager* mentioned practical concerns, to be sure—but not for the purpose of determining under what circumstances American courts could issue writs of *habeas corpus* for aliens abroad. It cited them to support its holding that the Constitution does not empower courts to issue writs of *habeas corpus* to aliens abroad in any circumstances. As Justice BLACK accurately said in dissent, "the Court's opinion inescapably denies courts power to afford the least bit of protection for any alien who is subject to our occupation government abroad, even if he is neither enemy nor belligerent and even after peace is officially declared." . . .

What drives today's decision is neither the meaning of the Suspension Clause, nor the principles of our precedents, but rather an inflated notion of judicial supremacy. The Court says that if the extraterritorial applicability of the Suspension Clause turned on formal notions of sovereignty, "it would be possible for the political branches to govern without legal constraint" in areas beyond the sovereign territory of the United States. That cannot be, the Court says, because it is the duty of this Court to say what the law is. . . . Our power "to say what the law is" is circumscribed by the limits of our statutorily and constitutionally conferred jurisdiction. And that is precisely the question in these cases: whether the Constitution confers *habeas* jurisdiction on federal courts to decide petitioners' claims. It is both irrational and arrogant to say that the answer must be yes, because otherwise we would not be supreme.

But so long as there are some places to which *habeas* does not run—so long as the Court's new "functional" test will not be satisfied in every case—

then there will be circumstances in which "it would be possible for the political branches to govern without legal constraint." Or, to put it more impartially, areas in which the legal determinations of the other branches will be (shudder!) supreme. In other words, judicial supremacy is not really assured by the constitutional rule that the Court creates. The gap between rationale and rule leads me to conclude that the Court's ultimate, unexpressed goal is to preserve the power to review the confinement of enemy prisoners held by the Executive anywhere in the world. The "functional" test usefully evades the precedential landmine of *Eisentrager* but is so inherently subjective that it clears a wide path for the Court to traverse in the years to come.

Putting aside the conclusive precedent of *Eisentrager*, it is clear that the original understanding of the Suspension Clause was that *habeas corpus* was not available to aliens abroad.

The Suspension Clause reads: "The Privilege of the Writ of *Habeas Corpus* shall not be suspended, unless when in Cases of Rebellion or Invasion the public Safety may require it." The proper course of constitutional interpretation is to give the text the meaning it was understood to have at the time of its adoption by the people. That course is especially demanded when (as here) the Constitution limits the power of Congress to infringe upon a pre-existing common-law right. The nature of the writ of *habeas corpus* that cannot be suspended must be defined by the common-law writ that was available at the time of the founding.

It is entirely clear that, at English common law, the writ of *habeas corpus* did not extend beyond the sovereign territory of the Crown. To be sure, the writ had an "extraordinary territorial ambit," because it was a so-called "prerogative writ," which, unlike other writs, could extend beyond the realm of England to other places where the Crown was sovereign.

But prerogative writs could not issue to foreign countries, even for British subjects; they were confined to the King's dominions—those areas over which the Crown was sovereign. Thus, the writ has never extended to Scotland, which, although united to England when James I succeeded to the English throne in 1603, was considered a foreign dominion under a different Crown—that of the King of Scotland.

The common-law writ was codified by the *Habeas Corpus* Act of 1679, which "stood alongside Magna Charta and the English Bill of Rights of 1689 as a towering common law lighthouse of liberty—a beacon by which framing lawyers in America consciously steered their course." The writ was established in the Colonies beginning in the 1690's and at least one colony adopted the 1679 Act almost verbatim. Section XI of the Act stated where the writ could run. It "may be directed and run into any county palatine, the cinque-ports, or other privileged places within the kingdom of England, dominion of Wales, or town of Berwick upon Tweed, and the islands of Jersey or Guernsey."

The Act did not extend the writ elsewhere, even though the existence of other places to which British prisoners could be sent was recognized by the Act....

In sum, all available historical evidence points to the conclusion that the writ would not have been available at common law for aliens captured and held outside the sovereign territory of the Crown....

Today the Court warps our Constitution in a way that goes beyond the narrow issue of the reach of the Suspension Clause, invoking judicially brainstormed separation-of-powers principles to establish a manipulable "functional" test for the extraterritorial reach of *habeas corpus* (and, no doubt, for the extra-territorial reach of other constitutional protections as well). It blatantly misdescribes important precedents, most conspicuously Justice JACKSON's opinion for the Court in *Johnson v. Eisentrager*. It breaks a chain of precedent as old as the common law that prohibits judicial inquiry into detentions of aliens abroad absent statutory authorization. And, most tragically, it sets our military commanders the impossible task of proving to a civilian court, under whatever standards this Court devises in the future, that evidence supports the confinement of each and every enemy prisoner.

The Nation will live to regret what the Court has done today. I dissent.

☐ *CHIEF JUSTICE ROBERTS, with whom Justice SCALIA, Justice THOMAS, and Justice ALITO join, dissenting.*

Today the Court strikes down as inadequate the most generous set of procedural protections ever afforded aliens detained by this country as enemy combatants. The political branches crafted these procedures amidst an ongoing military conflict, after much careful investigation and thorough debate. The Court rejects them today out of hand, without bothering to say what due process rights the detainees possess, without explaining how the statute fails to vindicate those rights, and before a single petitioner has even attempted to avail himself of the law's operation. And to what effect? The majority merely replaces a review system designed by the people's representatives with a set of shapeless procedures to be defined by federal courts at some future date. One cannot help but think, after surveying the modest practical results of the majority's ambitious opinion, that this decision is not really about the detainees at all, but about control of federal policy regarding enemy combatants.

The majority is adamant that the Guantanamo detainees are entitled to the protections of *habeas corpus*—its opinion begins by deciding that question. I regard the issue as a difficult one, primarily because of the unique and unusual jurisdictional status of Guantanamo Bay. I nonetheless agree with Justice SCALIA's analysis of our precedents and the pertinent history of the writ, and accordingly join his dissent. The important point for me, however, is that the Court should have resolved these cases on other grounds. *Habeas* is most fundamentally a procedural right, a mechanism for contesting the legality of executive detention. The critical threshold question in these cases, prior to any inquiry about the writ's scope, is whether the system the political branches designed protects whatever rights the detainees may possess. If so, there is no need for any additional process, whether called "*habeas*" or something else. . . .

I believe the system the political branches constructed adequately protects any constitutional rights aliens captured abroad and detained as enemy combatants may enjoy. I therefore would dismiss these cases on that ground. With all respect for the contrary views of the majority, I must dissent. . . .

■ IN COMPARATIVE PERSPECTIVE

The Supreme Court of Canada's 2008 Ruling on the Rights of Detainees

In 2007, the Supreme Court of Canada struck down a law authorizing the government to detain foreign-born terrorist suspects indefinitely in *R. v. Hape*, [2007] 2 S.C.R. 292, 2007 S.C.C. 26. Subsequently, in 2008 the Court held that the U.S. "regime" for detaining and interrogating a teenage Canadian in Guantanamo Bay since 2002 amounted to "a clear violation of fundamental human rights protected by international law," in *Canada v. Khadr*, 2008 SCC 28. The Court also ordered Canadian officials to disclose the records of interrogation of Omar Ahmed Khadr for the defense lawyers' use in defending him against war crimes charges made by the U.S. military. Khadr was captured in Afghanistan when he was fifteen years old and subsequently held in Guantanamo Bay.

The decision's conclusion that the detention and questioning of Khadr was illegal rested on the rulings of the U.S. Supreme Court in *Rasul v. Bush*, 542 U.S. 466 (2004) (excerpted in Vol. 1, Ch. 3) and *Hamdan v. Rumsfeld*, 126 S.Ct. 2749 (2006) (excerpted in Vol. 1, Ch. 3). The court did not mention the developments following *Hamdan*, and Congress's passage of the Military Commissions Act of 2006. In the Court's words, "The process in place at the time Canadian officials interviewed Mr. Khadr and passed the fruits of the interviews on to U.S. officials has been found by the United States Supreme Court to violate U.S. domestic law and international human rights obligations to which Canada is a party." Because of that, the Canadian security agents who interrogated Khadr violated the Canadian Charter of Rights and Freedoms. Hence, it ordered the disclosure to defense counsel of all documents in Canadian government hands bearing on the war crimes charges that Khadr faces before a U.S. military commission. The remedy under the Charter, however, the court ruled, does not require that Khadr have access to completely unedited versions of the documents and interrogations. Unredacted copies of those materials, the court noted, had already been turned over to a Canadian judge. And that judge should now review the material and "decide which documents fall within the scope of the disclosure obligation." In doing so, the court stressed that what was ultimately disclosed depended on a "balancing of national security and other considerations" under Canada's laws of evidence.

■ The Development of Law

Electronic Surveillance and the Foreign Intelligence Surveillance Court

In 2008, Congress revised the Foreign Intelligence Surveillance Act, which was created to issue warrants for domestic spying cases related to espionage and terrorism. (See the related boxes in Vol. 1, Ch.3, and Vol. 2, Ch. 7.) It did so because of controversies over the Bush administration's bypassing the court and conducting warrantless searches of electronic communications. The major provisions of the law, which will expire in 2012, provide the following:

1. Telecommunication companies that assisted the government in warrantless surveillance on the Internet after the September 11, 2001, terrorist attacks are shielded from lawsuits for invasion of privacy.

2. Procedures for monitoring telephone calls and e-mails of foreigners must be approved by the Foreign Intelligence Surveillance Court and the government's surveillance on U.S. citizens, including those abroad, require that court's approval of individual warrants.

3. The government is prohibited from targeting a foreigner in order to secretly eavesdrop on a U.S. citizen's telephone calls and e-mails without court approval.

4. The government may conduct emergency eavesdropping without a court-approved warrant but must seek approval within one week.

4

The President as Chief Executive in Domestic Affairs

In its 2009–2010 term, the Roberts Court will consider whether Congress unconstitutionally delegated to the executive branch by creating the Public Company Accounting Oversight Board (PCAOB) and delegated powers of appointment and removal of its members to the Securities and Exchange Commission (SEC), in *Free Enterprise Fund v. Public Company Accounting Oversight Board* (No. 08-861). Congress enacted the Sarbanes-Oxley Act of 2002 in response to highly publicized accounting scandals. The law established a five-member PCAOB and gave it the power to regulate audits of public companies. PCAOB members are appointed by the SEC and are only removable by the SEC for cause. The Free Enterprise Fund (FEF) sought a declaratory judgment that the provisions of the law were unconstitutional in violating the separation of powers, the Appointments Clause, and the nondelegation doctrine. A federal district court upheld the law because PCAOB members are inferior officers and Congress provided intelligible standards for the agency to follow. The district noted that the Appointments Clause would be satisfied if PCAOB members were selected by the SEC chairman alone, but held the FEF lacked standing to sue on that issue. The court denied the FEF's petition for a rehearing and the FEF appealed to the Supreme Court, which granted review.

D | *Accountability and Immunities*

In its 2008–2009 term, the Court considered the matter of qualified immunity from lawsuits against members of the president's cabinet and other high federal officials for alleged constitutional violations. The case, *Ashcroft v. Iqbal*; 129 S.Ct. 1937 (2009) stems from a suit against former Attorney General John D. Ashcroft and current Federal Bureau of Investigation (FBI) director Robert Mueller, among others, based on federal actions during the roundup and detention of men of Arab descent or identified with the Muslim faith, in the aftermath of the terrorists' attacks on September 11, 2001. Javiad Iqbal and others were detained by the FBI and held in a maximum-security facility, where he alleged that his constitutional rights were violated based on unlawful racial and religious discrimination. A federal district granted most of the defendants' motions to dismiss the suit based on their claims of qualified immunity. That decision was for the most part affirmed by the Court of Appeals for the Second Circuit, which reasoned that government officials are entitled to qualified immunity if they didn't clearly violate the law, or if they objectively and reasonably believed their actions did not violate the law. Subsequently, Iqbal was cleared of any alleged involvement in terrorism, but pled guilty to Social Security fraud and, after a year in prison, was deported to Pakistan. On appeal the Supreme Court split five to four in holding that high government officials cannot be held responsible for actions of subordinates and are liable for only their own personal misconduct. Writing for the majority, Justice Kennedy in this case determined personal liability for alleged torture had not been established. Justices Souter and Breyer filed dissenting opinions, which Justices Stevens and Ginsburg joined.

7

THE STATES AND AMERICAN FEDERALISM

A | States' Power over Commerce and Regulation

■ THE DEVELOPMENT OF LAW

Other Rulings on State Regulatory Powers in Alleged Conflict with Federal Legislation

CASE	VOTE	RULING
Rowe v. New Hampshire Motor Transportation Association, 128 S.Ct. 989 (2008)	9:0	Writing for the Court, Justice Breyer held that provisions of the Federal Aviation Administration Authorization Act (FAAAA) pre-

empted Maine's law requiring tobacco shippers to verify that the buyer was of legal age and prohibiting unlicensed tobacco shipments from out of state. Several other states have similar laws aimed at cutting down on the delivery of cigarettes bought over the Internet.

Wyeth v. Levine, 129 S.Ct. 1187 (2009)   6:3   Writing for the Court, Justice Stevens held that the Food, Drug, and Cosmetic Act (FDCA) labeling requirements for drugs do not preempt state court tort claims against drug manufacturers for failure to fully warn about potential harms of the usage of a drug. Chief Justice Roberts and Justices Scalia and Alito dissented.

Cuomo v. Clearing House Association, 129 S.Ct. 2710 (2009)   5:4   Writing for the Court, Justice Scalia held that under the 1864 National Bank Act, "visitorial" powers preempt a state attorney from issuing executive subpoenas in order to enforce state-free lending laws against national banks, though not the state's power of law enforcement. Justice Thomas issued a separate opinion, in part concurring and dissenting, which was joined by Chief Justice Roberts and Justices Kennedy and Alito.

Preston v. Ferrer, 128 S.Ct. 978 (2008)   8:1   Writing for the Court, Justice Ginsburg held that the Federal Arbitration Act preempts a state law that would refer a dispute to an administrative agency. Justice Thomas dissented.

Riegel v. Medtronic, 128 S.Ct. 999 (2008)   8:1   Writing for the Court, Chief Justice Roberts held that the Medical Device Amendments preemption clause overrides state common law claims against producers of medical devices that were approved by the Food and Drug Administration. Justice Ginsburg dissented.

Chamber of Commerce of the United States of America v. Brown, 128 S.Ct. 2408 (2008)   7:2   The majority held that the National Labor Relations Act as amended by the Taft-Hartley Act of 1947 preempted a California law that prohibited employers who receive state grants of more than $10,000 per year from using the money "to assist, promote, or deter union organizing." Writing for the Court, Justice Stevens held that federal law demonstrated a "congressional intent to encourage free debate on issues dividing labor and management." Justices Ginsburg and Breyer dissented.

Altria Group, Inc. v. Good, 129 S.Ct. 538 (2008)   5:4   Writing for a bare majority, Justice Stevens held that the Federal Cigarette Labeling and Advertising Act, which prohibits states from placing "smoking and health" requirements on cigarette advertisements, does not preempt suits against tobacco manufacturers for deceptive advertising. The Altria Group was sued under Maine's Unfair Trade Practices Act for fraudulently advertising that their "light" cigarettes delivered less tar and nicotine than regular brands. Justice Stevens emphasized that such suits are "predicated on the duty not to deceive" and thus are separate from the federal government's regulation of warnings on cigarette packs. Chief Justice Roberts and Justices Scalia and Alito joined Justice Thomas's dissent.

■ THE DEVELOPMENT OF LAW

Other Rulings on State Regulation of Commerce in the Absence of Federal Legislation

CASE	VOTE	RULING
Department of Revenue of Kentucky v. Davis, **128 S.Ct. 1801 (2008)**	7:2	The Court upheld Kentucky's law exempting interest on bonds issued by the state from taxation, while permitting the taxing of

interest on out-of-state bonds. Writing for the Court, Justice Souter held that while the dormant commerce clause bars "economic protectionism," regulations that benefit in-state economic interests by burdening out-of-state competitors, here the state's interests in financing its own civic responsibilities and state autonomy, outweighed the claim of economic protectionism. Justice Stevens and Thomas filed concurring opinions, while Justices Kennedy and Alito dissented, and Chief Justice Roberts and Justice Scalia filed separate opinions concurring in part.

8

REPRESENTATIVE GOVERNMENT, VOTING RIGHTS, AND ELECTORAL POLITICS

A | *Representative Government and the Franchise*

■ THE DEVELOPMENT OF LAW

Other Rulings Interpreting the Voting Rights Act

CASE	VOTE	RULING
Northwest Austin Municipal Utility District No. 1 v. Holder, 129 S.Ct. 2504 (2009)	8:1	Although declining to declare unconstitutional the 2006 extension of Section 5 of the voting Rights Act of 1965, which re-

quires Department of Justice preclearance of changes in election procedures in southern states and some counties in Alaska, California, Florida, Michigan, and elsewhere that once discriminated against minority voters, the Court held that a Texas utility district, which does not register voters, could apply

---

for a "bailout" under Section 4 of the law from the required Section 5 pre-clearance review if they could demonstrate that they had not recently engaged in voter discrimination, but also invited further constitutional challenges to law. Writing for the Court, Chief Justice Roberts observed: "more than forty years ago, this Court concluded that 'exceptional conditions' prevailing in certain parts of the country justified extraordinary legislation otherwise unfamiliar to our federal system. In part due to the success of that legislation, we are now a very different Nation. Whether conditions continue to justify such legislation is a difficult constitutional question we do not answer today." When extending the Voting Rights Act in 2006, Congress relied on evidence of voter discrimination that was decades old and offered no evidence of the persistence of such discrimination. Dissenting, Justice Clarence Thomas would have struck down Section 5 as unconstitutional, observing:

> The extensive pattern of discrimination that led the Court to previously uphold Section 5 as enforcing the Fifteenth Amendment no longer exists. Covered jurisdictions are not now engaged in a systematic campaign to deny black citizens access to the ballot through intimidation and violence. . . . Punishment for long past sins is not a legitimate basis for imposing a forward-looking preventative measure that has already served its purpose. Those supporting Section 5's reenactment argue that without it these jurisdictions would return to the racially discriminatory practices of thirty and forty years ago. But there is no evidence that public officials stand ready, if given the chance, to again engage in concerted acts of violence, terror, and subterfuge in order to keep minorities from voting. . . . Admitting that a prophylactic law as broad as Section 5 is no longer constitutionally justified based on current evidence of discrimination is not a sign of defeat. It is an acknowledgement of victory.

B | *Voting Rights and the Reapportionment Revolution*

In the 2008–2009 term, the Court handed down an important decision interpreting the application of the Voting Rights Act to racial redistricting. In *Bartlett v. Strickland* (2009) (summarized in the box that follows), the Court held that Section 2 of the Voting Rights Act does not require states to redraw voting district lines to allow racial minorities from other districts to cross over in order to vote in a district when the minority group in that district constitutes less than 50 percent of the population.

■ The Development of Law

Other Post–Shaw v. Reno Rulings on Racial Gerrymandering

CASE	VOTE	RULING
Bartlett v. Strtickland, 129 S.Ct. 1231 (2009)	5:4	Writing for a plurality, Justice Kennedy held that Section 2 of the Voting Rights Act does not

require states to redraw voting district lines to allow racial minorities from other districts to cross over in order to vote in a district when the minority group in that district constitutes less than 50 percent of the population. In spite of North Carolina's constitutional "whole county" provision prohibiting the general assembly from dividing counties when redrawing legislative districts, in 1991 the legislature redrew House District 18 to include portions of four counties, including Pender County, which at the time was a geographically compact majority-minority voting district. However, when that district was to be redrawn in 2003, the African American population had fallen below 50 percent, and instead of redrawing Pender County whole, the legislature split the district and crossed over portions of other districts. As a result, District 18 African American voting age population was 39.36 percent, whereas if Pender County's district had remained whole it would have had an African American voting age population of 35.33 percent. The rationale was that splitting Pender County gave African American voters the potential to elect a minority group's candidate, while leaving Pender County whole would have violated Section 2 of the Voting Rights Act. Justice Kennedy's words were, "There is an underlying principle of fundamental importance: We must be most cautious before interpreting a statute to require courts to make inquiries based on racial classifications and race-based predictions," though he added that "Racial discrimination and racially polarized voting are not ancient history. . . . Much remains to be done to ensure that citizens of all races have equal opportunity to share and participate in our democratic processes and traditions." By contrast, concurring Justice Thomas, joined by Justice Scalia, contended that the Voting Rights Act does not authorize any claim by minority voters; their influence is diluted in redistricting, no matter the size of the minority. Justices Stevens, Souter, Ginsburg, and Breyer dissented.

C | Campaigns and Elections

In its 2008–2009 term, the Court held that an Idaho law prohibiting payroll deductions for "political activities" does not violate the First Amendment by restricting speech in nonpublic forums in *Ysursa v. Pocatello Educational Association*, 129 S.Ct. 1093 (2009) (see The Development of Law box in this section). The Pocatello Educational Association sued the state of Idaho over the Voluntary Contribution Act, arguing that it burdened First Amendment protected "political speech." The term "political activities" in law includes virtually all types of electioneering and spending in support of or against candidates, ballot measures, and political parties. In the district court, the state conceded that all of the challenged provisions were unconstitutional, except for the one that prohibits payroll deductions for "political activities." The district court held that that provision was constitutional as applied to state employees but unconstitutional as applied to private and local government employees. The Court of Appeals for the Ninth Circuit held that the provision as applied to local government employees violated the First Amendment, but the Supreme Court reversed it by a six-to-three vote.

By five-to-four vote in *Davis v. Federal Election Commission*, 128 S.Ct. 2759 (2008), the Court invalidated Section 319, the so-called Millionaires' Amendment to the Bipartisan Campaign Reform Act of 2002 (BCRA), for violating the First and Fifth Amendments. The Millionaires' Amendment provided equalizing advantages to a candidate relying primarily on contributed funds who campaigns against a self-financed candidate. House of Representatives candidate Jack Davis challenged the law in federal district court in anticipation that his personal expenditures would exceed the statutory limitation in an upcoming election. Davis claims that the provision violated his First and Fifth Amendment rights through its disclosure requirements and contribution limitations. Under the law, a candidate for the House who spent more than $350,000 of his or her own money triggered additional reporting requirements and permitted the candidate's opponents to solicit three times the normal limit of $2,300 per contributor and granted greater spending by the opponent's party in behalf of the candidate. Writing for the majority, Justice Alito held that the provisions forced self-financed candidates "to choose between the right to engage in unfettered political speech and subjection to discriminatory fund raising levels," and that "the resulting drag on First Amendment right is not unconstitutional." Justices Stevens and Ginsburg issued separate opinions, in part concurring and dissenting, which Justices Souter and Breyer joined. The decision invites further challenges to state laws, such as Arizona's, North Carolina's, and Maine's, that penalize private funding of elections and promote public funding of campaigns.

In its 2007–2008 term, another sharply fragmented Court, however, upheld by a six-to-three vote Indiana's law requiring voters to produce a photo identification before casting a ballot in an election. Writing for a plurality and delivering the opinion for the Court in *Crawford v. Marion County Election Board* (excerpted below), Justice Stevens rejected a Fourteenth Amendment and Voting Rights Act challenge to the law, based on its discriminatory effect on the poor, the elderly, and the disabled. Justice Scalia,, joined by Justices Thomas and Alito, filed a concurring opinion. Justices Souter and Breyer filed separate dissenting opinions; Justice Ginsburg joined the former's dissent.

In its 2008–2009 term, the Roberts Court declined to decide but instead chose to carry over to its 2009–2010 term *Citizens United v. Federal Election Commission* for reargument. The case involves a challenge to the applilcation of the so-called McCain-Feingold campaign finance reform act, the Bipartisan Campaign Reform Act of 2002 (BCRA). That law was challenged in *McConnell v. Federal Election Commission*, 540 U.S. 93 (2003) (excerpted in Vol. 1, Ch. 3) and sharply divided the Rehnquist Court. At issue in *Citizens United* is whether a conservative group's distribution of a ninety-minute political film called *Hillary: The Movie*, attacking Senator Hillary Clinton's bid for the presidency in 2008, ran afoul of the BCRA or is protected by the First Amendment.

Crawford v. Marion County Election Board
128 S.Ct. 1610 (2008)

The Roberts Court weighed into the controversy between Republicans and Democrats over requiring government-issued photo identification as a precondition for voting in elections. In 2005 the Republican-controlled legislature in Indiana enacted a law requiring voters to provide a photo identification before casting a ballot on the ground that it counters voter fraud and political corruption. Besides Indiana, six other states—Florida, Georgia, Hawaii, Louisiana, Michigan, and South Dakota—have similar laws, and two dozen other states were considering such legislation. Democrats immediately challenged the law for disadvantaging the poor, the elderly, and the disabled, on the ground that it violated the Fourteenth Amendment and the Voting Rights Act. A federal district court upheld the statute and its decision was affirmed by the Court of Appeals for the Seventh Circuit. That decision was appealed and the Supreme Court granted review.

The appellate court's decision was affirmed by a six-to-three vote. Justice Stevens delivered the opinion for the Court, which commanded only the votes of Chief Justice Roberts and Justice Kennedy. Justice Scalia filed a concurring opinion, which Justices Thomas and Alito joined. Justices Breyer and Souter filed dissenting opinions, and Justice Ginsburg joined the latter's dissent.

☐ *Justice STEVENS announced the judgment of the Court and delivered an opinion in which THE CHIEF JUSTICE and Justice KENNEDY join.*

At issue in these cases is the constitutionality of an Indiana statute requiring citizens voting in person on election day, or casting a ballot in person at the office of the circuit court clerk prior to election day, to present photo identification issued by the government.

Referred to as either the "Voter ID Law" or "SEA 483," the statute applies to in-person voting at both primary and general elections. The requirement does not apply to absentee ballots submitted by mail, and the statute contains an exception for persons living and voting in a state-licensed facility such as a nursing home. A voter who is indigent or has a religious objection to being photographed may cast a provisional ballot that will be counted only if she executes an appropriate affidavit before the circuit court clerk within 10 days following the election. A voter who has photo identification but is unable to present that identification on election day may file a provisional ballot that will be counted if she brings her photo identification to the circuit county clerk's office within 10 days. No photo identification is required in order to register to vote, and the State offers free photo identification to qualified voters able to establish their residence and identity. . . .

In *Harper v. Virginia Bd. of Elections,* 383 U.S. 663 (1966), the Court held that Virginia could not condition the right to vote in a state election on the payment of a poll tax of $1.50. We rejected the dissenters' argument that the interest in promoting civic responsibility by weeding out those voters who did not care enough about public affairs to pay a small sum for the privilege of voting provided a rational basis for the tax. Applying a stricter standard, we concluded that a State "violates the Equal Protection Clause of the Fourteenth Amendment whenever it makes the affluence of the voter or payment of any fee an electoral standard." We used the term "invidiously discriminate" to describe conduct prohibited under that standard, noting that we had previously held that while a State may obviously impose "reasonable residence restrictions on the availability of the ballot," it "may not deny the opportunity to vote to a bona fide resident merely because he is a member of the armed services." Although the State's justification for the tax was rational, it was invidious because it was irrelevant to the voter's qualifications.

Thus, under the standard applied in *Harper,* even rational restrictions on the right to vote are invidious if they are unrelated to voter qualifications. In *Anderson v. Celebrezze,* 460 U.S. 780 (1983), however, we confirmed the general rule that "evenhanded restrictions that protect the integrity and reliability of the electoral process itself" are not invidious and satisfy the standard set forth in *Harper.* Rather than applying any "litmus test" that would neatly separate valid from invalid restrictions, we concluded that a court must identify and evaluate the interests put forward by the State as justifications for the burden imposed by its rule, and then make the "hard judgment" that our adversary system demands.

In later election cases we have followed *Anderson*'s balancing approach. Thus, in *Norman v. Reed,* 502 U.S. 279 (1992), after identifying the burden Illinois imposed on a political party's access to the ballot, we "called for the demonstration of a corresponding interest sufficiently weighty to justify the limitation," and concluded that the "severe restriction" was not justified by a narrowly drawn state interest of compelling importance. Later, in *Burdick v. Takushi,* 504 U.S. 428 (1992), we applied *Anderson*'s standard for "'reasonable, nondiscriminatory restrictions,'" and upheld Hawaii's prohibition on write-in voting despite the fact that it prevented a significant number of "voters from participating in Hawaii elections in a meaningful manner." We reaffirmed *Anderson*'s requirement that a court evaluating a constitutional challenge to an election regulation weigh the asserted injury to the right to vote against the "'precise interests put forward by the State as justifications for the burden imposed by its rule.'"

In neither *Norman* nor *Burdick* did we identify any litmus test for measuring the severity of a burden that a state law imposes on a political party, an individual voter, or a discrete class of voters. However slight that burden may appear, as *Harper* demonstrates, it must be justified by relevant and legitimate state interests "sufficiently weighty to justify the limitation." We therefore begin our analysis of the constitutionality of Indiana's statute by focusing on those interests.

The State has identified several state interests that arguably justify the burdens that SEA 483 imposes on voters and potential voters. While petitioners argue that the statute was actually motivated by partisan concerns and dispute both the significance of the State's interests and the magnitude of any real threat to those interests, they do not question the legitimacy of the interests the State has identified. Each is unquestionably relevant to the State's interest in protecting the integrity and reliability of the electoral process.

The first is the interest in deterring and detecting voter fraud. The State has a valid interest in participating in a nationwide effort to improve and modernize election procedures that have been criticized as antiquated and inefficient. . . . In the National Voter Registration Act of 1993 (NVRA) Congress established procedures that would both increase the number of registered voters and protect the integrity of the electoral process. The statute requires state motor vehicle driver's license applications to serve as voter registration applications. While that requirement has increased the number of registered voters, the statute also contains a provision restricting States' ability to remove names from the lists of registered voters. These protections have been partly responsible for inflated lists of registered voters. . . .

The only kind of voter fraud that SEA 483 addresses is in-person voter impersonation at polling places. The record contains no evidence of any such fraud actually occurring in Indiana at any time in its history. Moreover, petitioners argue that provisions of the Indiana Criminal Code punishing such conduct as a felony provide adequate protection against the risk that such conduct will occur in the future. It remains true, however, that flagrant examples of such fraud in other parts of the country have been documented throughout this Nation's history by respected historians and journalists, that occasional examples have surfaced in recent years, and that Indiana's own experience with fraudulent voting in the 2003 Democratic primary for East Chicago Mayor—though perpetrated using absentee ballots and not in-person fraud—demonstrate that not only is the risk of voter fraud real but that it could affect the outcome of a close election.

There is no question about the legitimacy or importance of the State's interest in counting only the votes of eligible voters. Moreover, the interest in orderly administration and accurate recordkeeping provides a sufficient justification for carefully identifying all voters participating in the election process. While the most effective method of preventing election fraud may well be debatable, the propriety of doing so is perfectly clear. . . .

Finally, the State contends that it has an interest in protecting public confidence "in the integrity and legitimacy of representative government." While that interest is closely related to the State's interest in preventing voter fraud, public confidence in the integrity of the electoral process has independent significance, because it encourages citizen participation in the democratic process. States employ different methods of identifying eligible voters at the polls. Some merely check off the names of registered voters who identify themselves; others require voters to present registration cards or other documentation before they can vote; some require voters to sign their names so their signatures can be compared with those on file; and in recent years an increasing number of States have relied primarily on photo identification. A photo identification requirement imposes some burdens on voters that other methods of identification do not share. For example, a voter may lose his photo identification, may have his wallet stolen on the way to the polls, or may not resemble the photo in the identification because he recently grew a beard. Burdens of that sort arising from life's vagaries, however, are neither so serious nor so frequent as to raise any question about the constitutionality of SEA 483; the availability of the right to cast a provisional ballot provides an adequate remedy for problems of that character.

The burdens that are relevant to the issue before us are those imposed on persons who are eligible to vote but do not possess a current photo identification that complies with the requirements of SEA 483. The fact that most voters already possess a valid driver's license, or some other form of acceptable identification, would not save the statute under our reasoning in *Harper*, if the State required voters to pay a tax or a fee to obtain a new photo identification. But just as other States provide free voter registration cards, the photo identification cards issued by Indiana's BMV are also free. For most voters who need them, the inconvenience of making a trip to the BMV, gathering the required documents, and posing for a photograph surely does not qualify as a substantial burden on the right to vote, or even represent a significant increase over the usual burdens of voting.

Both evidence in the record and facts of which we may take judicial notice, however, indicate that a somewhat heavier burden may be placed on a limited number of persons. They include elderly persons born out-of-state, who may have difficulty obtaining a birth certificate; persons who because of economic or other personal limitations may find it difficult either to secure a copy of their birth certificate or to assemble the other required documentation to obtain a state-issued identification; homeless persons; and persons with a religious objection to being photographed. If we assume, as the evidence suggests, that some members of these classes were registered voters when SEA 483 was enacted, the new identification requirement may have imposed a special burden on their right to vote.

The severity of that burden is, of course, mitigated by the fact that, if eligible, voters without photo identification may cast provisional ballots that will ultimately be counted. To do so, however, they must travel to the circuit court clerk's office within 10 days to execute the required affidavit. It is unlikely that such a requirement would pose a constitutional problem unless it is wholly unjustified. And even assuming that the burden may not be justified as to a few voters, that conclusion is by no means sufficient to establish petitioners' right to the relief they seek in this litigation. . . .

[If] a nondiscriminatory law is supported by valid neutral justifications, those justifications should not be disregarded simply because partisan interests may have provided one motivation for the votes of individual legislators. The state interests identified as justifications for SEA 483 are both neutral and sufficiently strong to require us to reject petitioners' facial attack on the statute. The application of the statute to the vast majority of Indiana voters is amply justified by the valid interest in protecting "the integrity and reliability of the electoral process." *Anderson.*

☐ *Justice SCALIA, with whom Justice THOMAS and Justice ALITO join, concurring in the judgment.*

The lead opinion assumes petitioners' premise that the voter-identification law "may have imposed a special burden on" some voters, but holds that petitioners have not assembled evidence to show that the special burden is severe enough to warrant strict scrutiny. That is true enough, but for the sake of clarity and finality (as well as adherence to precedent), I prefer to decide these cases on the grounds that petitioners' premise is irrelevant and that the burden at issue is minimal and justified.

To evaluate a law respecting the right to vote—whether it governs voter qualifications, candidate selection, or the voting process—we use the approach set out in *Burdick v. Takushi*, 504 U.S. 428 (1992). This calls for application of a deferential "important regulatory interests" standard for nonsevere, nondiscriminatory restrictions, reserving strict scrutiny for laws that severely restrict the right to vote. The lead opinion resists the import of *Burdick* by characterizing it as simply adopting "the balancing approach" of *Anderson v. Celebrezze*, 460 U.S. 780 (1983). Although *Burdick* liberally quoted *Anderson*, *Burdick* forged *Anderson's* amorphous "flexible standard" into something resembling an administrable rule.

Since *Burdick*, we have repeatedly reaffirmed the primacy of its two-track approach. Of course, we have to identify a burden before we can weigh it. The Indiana law affects different voters differently, but what petitioners view as the law's several light and heavy burdens are no more than the different impacts of the single burden that the law uniformly imposes on all voters. To vote in person in Indiana, everyone must have and present a photo identification that can be obtained for free. The State draws no classifications, let alone discriminatory ones, except to establish optional absentee and provisional balloting for certain poor, elderly, and institutionalized voters and for religious objectors. Nor are voters who already have photo identifications exempted from the burden, since those voters must maintain the accuracy of the information displayed on the identifications, renew them before they expire, and replace them if they are lost.

The Indiana photo-identification law is a generally applicable, nondiscriminatory voting regulation, and our precedents refute the view that individual impacts are relevant to determining the severity of the burden it imposes. . . .

Not all of our decisions predating *Burdick* addressed whether a challenged voting regulation severely burdened the right to vote, but when we began to grapple with the magnitude of burdens, we did so categorically and did not consider the peculiar circumstances of individual voters or candidates.

Insofar as our election-regulation cases rest upon the requirements of the Fourteenth Amendment, weighing the burden of a nondiscriminatory voting law upon each voter and concomitantly requiring exceptions for vulnerable voters would effectively turn back decades of equal-protection jurisprudence. A voter complaining about such a law's effect on him has no valid equal-protection claim because, without proof of discriminatory intent, a generally applicable law with disparate impact is not unconstitutional.

Even if I thought that *stare decisis* did not foreclose adopting an individual-focused approach, I would reject it as an original matter. This is an area where the dos and don'ts need to be known in advance of the election, and voter-by-voter examination of the burdens of voting regulations would prove especially disruptive. . . .

[D]etailed judicial supervision of the election process would flout the Constitution's express commitment of the task to the States. It is for state legislatures to weigh the costs and benefits of possible changes to their election codes, and their judgment must prevail unless it imposes a severe and unjustified overall burden upon the right to vote, or is intended to disadvantage a particular class. Judicial review of their handiwork must apply an objective, uniform standard that will enable them to determine whether the burden they impose is too severe.

The lead opinion's record-based resolution of these cases, which neither rejects nor embraces the rule of our precedents, provides no certainty, and will embolden litigants who surmise that our precedents have been abandoned. There is no good reason to prefer that course. The universally applicable requirements of Indiana's voter-identification law are eminently reasonable. The burden of acquiring, possessing, and showing a free photo identification is simply not severe, because it does not "even represent a significant increase over the usual burdens of voting." And the State's interests are sufficient to sustain that minimal burden. That should end the matter. . . .

□ *Justice BREYER, dissenting.*

Indiana's statute requires registered voters to present photo identification at the polls. It imposes a burden upon some voters, but it does so in order to prevent fraud, to build confidence in the voting system, and thereby to maintain the integrity of the voting process. In determining whether this statute violates the Federal Constitution, I would balance the voting-related interests that the statute affects, asking "whether the statute burdens any one such interest in a manner out of proportion to the statute's salutary effects upon the others (perhaps, but not necessarily, because of the existence of a clearly superior, less restrictive alternative)." *Nixon v. Shrink Missouri Government PAC,* 528 U.S. 377 (2000) (BREYER, J., concurring). Applying this standard, I believe the statute is unconstitutional because it imposes a disproportionate burden upon those eligible voters who lack a driver's license or other statutorily valid form of photo ID.

Like Justice STEVENS, I give weight to the fact that a national commission, chaired by former President Jimmy Carter and former Secretary of State James Baker, studied the issue and recommended that States should require voter photo IDs. (Carter-Baker Report). Because the record does not discredit the Carter-Baker Report or suggest that Indiana is exceptional, I see nothing to prevent Indiana's Legislature (or a federal court considering the constitutionality of the statute) from taking account of the legislatively relevant facts the report sets forth and paying attention to its expert conclusions. Thus, I share the general view of the lead opinion insofar as it holds that the Constitution does not automatically forbid Indiana from enacting a photo ID requirement. Were I also to believe, as Justice STEVENS believes, that the burden imposed by the Indiana statute on eligible voters who lack photo IDs is indeterminate "on the basis of the record that has been made in this litigation," or were I to believe, as Justice SCALIA believes, that the burden the statute imposes is "minimal" or "justified," then I too would reject the petitioners' facial attack, primarily for the reasons set forth in . . . the lead opinion.

I cannot agree, however, with Justice STEVENS' or Justice SCALIA's assessment of the burdens imposed by the statute. The Carter-Baker Commission conditioned its recommendation upon the States' willingness to ensure that the requisite photo IDs "be easily available and issued free of charge" and that the requirement be "phased in" over two federal election cycles, to ease the transition. . . . Indiana's law fails to satisfy these aspects of the Commission's recommendation.

For one thing, an Indiana nondriver, most likely to be poor, elderly, or disabled, will find it difficult and expensive to travel to the Bureau of Motor Vehicles, particularly if he or she resides in one of the many Indiana counties lacking a public transportation system. For another, many of these individuals may be uncertain about how to obtain the underlying documentation, usually a passport or a birth certificate, upon which the statute insists. And some may find the costs associated with these documents unduly burdensome (up to $12 for a copy of a birth certificate; up to $100 for a passport). By way of comparison, this Court previously found unconstitutionally burdensome a poll tax of $1.50 (less than $10 today, inflation-adjusted). See *Harper v. Virginia Bd. of Elections*, 383 U.S. 663 (1966). Further, Indiana's exception for voters who cannot afford this cost imposes its own burden: a postelection trip to the county clerk or county election board to sign an indigency affidavit after each election.

By way of contrast, two other States—Florida and Georgia—have put into practice photo ID requirements significantly less restrictive than Indiana's. Under the Florida law, the range of permissible forms of photo ID is substantially greater than in Indiana (including employee badge or ID, a debit or credit card, a student ID, a retirement center ID, a neighborhood association ID, and a public assistance ID). Moreover, a Florida voter who lacks photo ID may cast a provisional ballot at the polling place that will be counted if the State determines that his signature matches the one on his voter registration form.

Georgia restricts voters to a more limited list of acceptable photo IDs than does Florida, but accepts in addition to proof of voter registration a broader range of underlying documentation than does Indiana. . . .

For these reasons, I dissent.

☐ *Justice SOUTER, with whom Justice GINSBURG joins, dissenting.*

Indiana's "Voter ID Law"delete threatens to impose nontrivial burdens on the voting right of tens of thousands of the State's citizens, and a significant percentage of those individuals are likely to be deterred from voting. The statute is unconstitutional under the balancing standard of *Burdick v. Takushi*, 504 U.S. 428 (1992): a State may not burden the right to vote merely by invoking abstract interests, be they legitimate or even compelling, but must make a particular, factual showing that threats to its interests outweigh the particular impediments it has imposed. The State has made no such justification here, and as to some aspects of its law, it has hardly even tried. I therefore respectfully dissent from the Court's judgment sustaining the statute.

Voting-rights cases raise two competing interests, the one side being the fundamental right to vote. As against the unfettered right, however, lies the "[c]ommon sense, as well as constitutional law . . . that government must play an active role in structuring elections; 'as a practical matter, there must be a substantial regulation of elections if they are to be fair and honest and if some sort of order, rather than chaos, is to accompany the democratic processes.'" *Burdick.*

Given the legitimacy of interests on both sides, we have avoided pre-set levels of scrutiny in favor of a sliding-scale balancing analysis: the scrutiny varies with the effect of the regulation at issue. And whatever the claim, the

Court has long made a careful, ground-level appraisal both of the practical burdens on the right to vote and of the State's reasons for imposing those precise burdens. Thus, in *Burdick*: "A court considering [such] a challenge . . . must weigh 'the character and magnitude of the asserted injury to the rights protected by the First and Fourteenth Amendments that the plaintiff seeks to vindicate' against 'the precise interests put forward by the State as justifications for the burden imposed by its rule,' taking into consideration 'the extent to which those interests make it necessary to burden the plaintiff's rights.' " But I think it does not insist enough on the hard facts that our standard of review demands. . . .

The first set of burdens shown in these cases is the travel costs and fees necessary to get one of the limited variety of federal or state photo identifications needed to cast a regular ballot under the Voter ID Law. The travel is required for the personal visit to a license branch of the Indiana Bureau of Motor Vehicles (BMV), which is demanded of anyone applying for a driver's license or nondriver photo identification. . . .

Although making voters travel farther than what is convenient for most and possible for some does not amount to a "severe" burden under *Burdick*, that is no reason to ignore the burden altogether. It translates into an obvious economic cost (whether in work time lost, or getting and paying for transportation) that an Indiana voter must bear to obtain an ID. For those voters who can afford the roundtrip, a second financial hurdle appears: in order to get photo identification for the first time, they need to present " 'a birth certificate, a certificate of naturalization, U.S. veterans photo identification, U.S. military photo identification, or a U.S. passport.' " As the lead opinion says, the two most common of these documents come at a price: Indiana counties charge anywhere from $3 to $12 for a birth certificate (and in some other States the fee is significantly higher), and that same price must usually be paid for a first-time passport, since a birth certificate is required to prove U.S. citizenship by birth. The total fees for a passport, moreover, are up to about $100. So most voters must pay at least one fee to get the ID necessary to cast a regular ballot. As with the travel costs, these fees are far from shocking on their face, but in the *Burdick* analysis it matters that both the travel costs and the fees are disproportionately heavy for, and thus disproportionately likely to deter, the poor, the old, and the immobile.

To be sure, Indiana has a provisional-ballot exception to the ID requirement for individuals the State considers "indigent" as well as those with religious objections to being photographed. . . .

[The] provisional ballots do not obviate the burdens of getting photo identification. And even if that were not so, the provisional-ballot option would be inadequate for a further reason: the indigency exception by definition offers no relief to those voters who do not consider themselves (or would not be considered) indigent but as a practical matter would find it hard, for nonfinancial reasons, to get the required ID (most obviously the disabled).

Indiana's Voter ID Law thus threatens to impose serious burdens on the voting right, even if not "severe" ones, and the next question under *Burdick* is whether the number of individuals likely to be affected is significant as well. Record evidence and facts open to judicial notice answer yes. Although the District Court found that petitioners failed to offer any reliable empirical study of numbers of voters affected, we may accept that court's rough calculation that 43,000 voting-age residents lack the kind of identification card required by Indiana's law. The District Court made that estimate by comparing BMV records reproduced in petitioners' statistician's report with U.S.

Census Bureau figures for Indiana's voting-age population in 2004, and the State does not argue that these raw data are unreliable. . . .

The upshot is this. Tens of thousands of voting-age residents lack the necessary photo identification. A large proportion of them are likely to be in bad shape economically. The Voter ID Law places hurdles in the way of either getting an ID or of voting provisionally, and they translate into nontrivial economic costs. There is accordingly no reason to doubt that a significant number of state residents will be discouraged or disabled from voting. . . .

There is no denying the abstract importance, the compelling nature, of combating voter fraud. But it takes several steps to get beyond the level of abstraction here. To begin with, requiring a voter to show photo identification before casting a regular ballot addresses only one form of voter fraud: in-person voter impersonation. The photo ID requirement leaves untouched the problems of absentee-ballot fraud, which (unlike in-person voter impersonation) is a documented problem in Indiana; of registered voters voting more than once (but maintaining their own identities) in different counties or in different States; of felons and other disqualified individuals voting in their own names; of vote buying; or, for that matter, of ballot-stuffing, ballot miscounting, voter intimidation, or any other type of corruption on the part of officials administering elections. And even the State's interest in deterring a voter from showing up at the polls and claiming to be someone he is not must, in turn, be discounted for the fact that the State has not come across a single instance of in-person voter impersonation fraud in all of Indiana's history. . . .

In sum, fraud by individuals acting alone, however difficult to detect, is unlikely. And while there may be greater incentives for organized groups to engage in broad-gauged in-person voter impersonation fraud, it is also far more difficult to conceal larger enterprises of this sort. The State's argument about the difficulty of detecting the fraud lacks real force. . . .

The State's asserted interests in modernizing elections and combating fraud are decidedly modest; at best, they fail to offset the clear inference that thousands of Indiana citizens will be discouraged from voting. The two remaining justifications, meanwhile, actually weaken the State's case.

The lead opinion agrees with the State that "the inflation of its voter rolls is further support for its enactment of" the Voter ID Law. This is a puzzling conclusion, given the fact, which the lead opinion notes, that the National Government filed a complaint against Indiana, containing this allegation: "Indiana has failed to conduct a general program that makes a reasonable effort to identify and remove ineligible voters from the State's registration list; has failed to remove such ineligible voters; and has failed to engage in oversight actions sufficient to ensure that local election jurisdictions identify and remove such ineligible voters." The Federal Government and the State agreed to settle the case, and a consent decree and order have been entered, requiring Indiana to fulfill its list-maintenance obligations under Sec. 8 of the National Voter Registration Act of 1993.

How any of this can justify restrictions on the right to vote is difficult to say. The State is simply trying to take advantage of its own wrong: if it is true that the State's fear of in-person voter impersonation fraud arises from its bloated voter checklist, the answer to the problem is in the State's own hands. The claim that the State has an interest in addressing a symptom of the problem (alleged impersonation) rather than the problem itself (the negligently maintained bloated rolls) is thus self-defeating; it shows that the State has no justifiable need to burden the right to vote as it does, and it suggests that the State is not as serious about combating fraud as it claims to be.

The State's final justification, its interest in safeguarding voter confidence, similarly collapses. The problem with claiming this interest lies in its connection to the bloated voter rolls; the State has come up with nothing to suggest that its citizens doubt the integrity of the State's electoral process, except its own failure to maintain its rolls. The answer to this problem is not to burden the right to vote, but to end the official negligence.

It should go without saying that none of this is to deny States' legitimate interest in safeguarding public confidence. The Court has, for example, recognized that fighting perceptions of political corruption stemming from large political contributions is a legitimate and substantial state interest, underlying not only campaign finance laws, but bribery and anti-gratuity statutes as well. But the force of the interest depends on the facts (or plausibility of the assumptions) said to justify invoking it. . . . Without a shred of evidence that in-person voter impersonation is a problem in the State, much less a crisis, Indiana has adopted one of the most restrictive photo identification requirements in the country. The State recognizes that tens of thousands of qualified voters lack the necessary federally issued or state-issued identification, but it insists on implementing the requirement immediately, without allowing a transition period for targeted efforts to distribute the required identification to individuals who need it.

The State hardly even tries to explain its decision to force indigents or religious objectors to travel all the way to their county seats every time they wish to vote, and if there is any waning of confidence in the administration of elections it probably owes more to the State's violation of federal election law than to any imposters at the polling places. It is impossible to say, on this record, that the State's interest in adopting its signally inhibiting photo identification requirement has been shown to outweigh the serious burdens it imposes on the right to vote. . . .

The Indiana Voter ID Law is thus unconstitutional: the state interests fail to justify the practical limitations placed on the right to vote, and the law imposes an unreasonable and irrelevant burden on voters who are poor and old. I would vacate the judgment of the Seventh Circuit, and remand for further proceedings.

■ THE DEVELOPMENT OF LAW

Other Rulings on Campaigns and Elections

CASE	VOTE	RULING
New York State Board of Elections v. Lopez Torres, 128 S.Ct. 791 (2008)	9:0	Writing for the Court, Justice Scalia upheld New York's process for selecting its supreme court justices through party conventions. Under the state law, each political party selects one candidate to run in the general election. That law was challenged as a violation of the First

Amendment freedom of association for discriminating against challengers to party-selected candidates. But the Court held that political parties have First Amendment protection to determine their own selection process and rejected the claims of candidates who do not have party leadership support.

Washington State Grange v.   7:2   Writing for the Court, Justice
Washington State Republican   Thomas upheld Washington State's
Party, 128 S.Ct. 1194 (2008)   law requiring candidates for elective office to be identified on the ballot by their self-designated "party preference." The majority held that the requirement did not unduly burden political parties' freedom of association under the First Amendment. Justices Scalia and Kennedy dissented.

Ysursa v. Pocatello Education   6:3   Writing for the Court, Chief Jus-
Association, 129 S.Ct. 1093   tice Roberts held that states may
(2009)   order local governments to forbid payroll deductions for union political activities and rejected the union's claim that that violated the First Amendment. In his words: "The First Amendment prohibits government from 'abridging the freedom of speech'; it does not confer an affirmative right to use government payroll mechanisms for the purpose of obtaining funds for expression."

Caperton v. A. T. Massey   6:3   By a five-to-four vote, the Court
Coal Co., 129 S.Ct. 2252   held that it is unconstitutional
(2009)   for a state supreme court justice to sit on a case involving the financial interests of a major donor to the justices election campaign. Writing for the majority, Justice Kennedy held that West Virginia Supreme Court Chief Justice Brent Benjamin should have recused himself from a case that overturned a $50-million verdict against a company headed by a man who contributed $3 million to the justice's election. The failure to do so ran afoul of the Due Process Clause, which incorporates the common-law rule requiring recusal when a judge has "a direct, personal, substantial, pecuniary interest" in a case. According to the Court's precedents, recusal is required where "the probability of actual bias on the part of the judge or decisionmaker is too high to be constitutionally tolerable." In Justice Kennedy's words: "Not every campaign contribution by a litigant or attorney creates a probability of bias that requires a judge's recusal, but this is an exceptional case." By contrast, dissenting Chief Justice Roberts, joined by Justices Scalia, Thomas, and Alito, countered that the ruling "requires state and federal judges simultaneously to act as political scientists (why did candidate X win the election?), economists (was the financial support disproportionate?), and psychologists (is there likely to be a debt of gratitude?)."

9

ECONOMIC RIGHTS AND AMERICAN CAPITALISM

C | *The "Takings Clause" and Just Compensation"*

In its 2009–2010 term, the Court will reconsider constitutional limits on states' power to restore storm-eroded beaches along the ocean and lakeshores, when such action infringes on private property lines, in *Stop the Beach Renourishment v. Florida* (Docket No. 08–1151). Florida's legislature enacted the Shore Preservation Act to establish procedures to restore eroded shorelines damaged by hurricanes. Stop the Beach Renourishment (STBR), a nonprofit association of owners of beachfront property, challenged the constitutionality of the beach restoration project. STBR claimed that a provision of the law pertaining to the shoreline boundary unconstitutionally deprived waterfront property owners of upland property rights without just compensation. A state appellate court held that the takings required eminent domain proceedings, but subsequently certified the question as having public importance since beach erosion posed a serious problem for the economy and general welfare of the public. The state supreme court reversed, ruling that the law fixing shoreline boundaries did not unconstitutionally deprive upland owners of their rights without just compensation.

SUPREME COURT WATCH 2009
VOLUME TWO

4

THE NATIONALIZATION OF THE BILL OF RIGHTS

B | *The Rise and Retreat of the "Due Process Revolution"*

■ THE DEVELOPMENT OF LAW

Other Recent Rulings on Substantive and Procedural Due Process

---

CASE	VOTE	RULING
Rivera v. Illinois, 129 S.Ct. 1446 (2009)	9:0	During jury selection for Michael Rivera's first-degree murder trial, his counsel sought to use a pe-

remptory challenge to excuse a venire member Deloris Gomez. Rivera had already used peremptory against women, and it was conceded that there was no basis to challenge Gomez for cause. The trial court rejected the peremptory challenge out of concern that it was discriminatory under *Batson v. Kentucky,* 476 U.S. 79 (1986) (see Vol. 2, Ch. 12), holding that parties may not use peremptory challenges to exclude jurors based on race, ethnicity, or gender. Writing for a unanimous Court, Justice Ginsburg held that even though

---

the trial court erred and the composed jury might have otherwise decided the case differently, because there was no juror removed for cause, Rivera's Sixth Amendment right to an impartial jury and Fourteenth Amendment right to due process was not violated. In short, due process does not meticulously observe state procedures, but only "the fundamental elements of fairness in a criminal trial."

Caperton v. A. T. Massey Coal Co., **129 S.Ct.** 2252 (2009)   5:4   By a five-to-four vote, the Court held that it is unconstitutional for a state supreme court justice to sit on a case involving the financial interests of a major donor to the justices election campaign. Writing for the majority, Justice Kennedy held that West Virginia Supreme Court Chief Justice Brent Benjamin should have recused himself from a case that overturned a $50-million verdict against a company headed by a man who contributed $3 million to the justice's election. The failure to do so ran afoul of the Due Process Clause, which incorporates the common-law rule requiring recusal when a judge has "a direct, personal, substantial, pecuniary interest" in a case. According to the Court's precedents, recusal is required where "the probability of actual bias on the part of the judge or decisionmaker is too high to be constitutionally tolerable." In Justice Kennedy's words: "Not every campaign contribution by a litigant or attorney creates a probability of bias that requires a judge's recusal, but this is an exceptional case." By contrast, dissenting Chief Justice Roberts, joined by Justices Scalia, Thomas, and Alito, countered that the ruling "requires state and federal judges simultaneously to act as political scientists (why did candidate X win the election?), economists (was the financial support disproportionate?), and psychologists (is there likely to be a debt of gratitude?)."

District Attorney's Office for Third District v. Osborne, **129 S.Ct.** 2308 (2009)   5:4   Alaska is one of three states that do not allow postconviction access to DNA and other biological evidence in order to challenge a defendant's conviction. Writing for a bare majority, Chief Justice Roberts rejected a due process challenge and observed that it was up to the states and Congress to decide who has a right to testing that might prove innocence after a conviction. In his words, "[The] challenges DNA technology poses to our criminal justice system and our traditional notions of finality" are better left to elected officials than federal judges. "To suddenly constitutionalize this area would short-circuit what looks to be a prompt and considered legislative response." Justices Stevens, Souter, Ginsburg, and Breyer dissented.

■ THE DEVELOPMENT OF LAW

The Supreme Court Rules on the Second Amendment Right to Keep and Bear Arms

In a historic ruling in *District of Columbia v. Heller,* 128 S.Ct. 2783(2008), the Court struck down two key provisions of the District of Columbia's 1976 ban on handguns, the strictest in the nation: (1) a flat ban on possessing a handgun in one's home; and (2) a requirement that any gun, except one kept at a business, must be unloaded and disassembled or have a trigger lock in place. The Court left intact other provisions, such as the requirement that guns must be registered and licensed. Not since *United States v. Miller,* 307 U.S. 174 (1939), had the Court addressed the amendment (see the Constitutional History box on the Second and Third Amendments in Vol. 2, Ch. 4). For the first time, the Court held that the Second Amendment (providing that "A well regulated Militia, being necessary to the security of a free State, the right of the people to keep and bear Arms, shall not be infringed") guarantees individuals the right to possess handguns in their homes.

Writing for a bare majority, Justice Scalia advanced several arguments— textualist, intratextualist, and based on the original understanding of the amendment—for invalidating the ban on handguns. First, he separated the prefatory and operative clauses of the amendment, observing that "The Second Amendment is naturally divided into two parts: its prefatory clause [A well regulated Militia] and its operative clause [the right of the people to keep and bear Arms] . . . [A] prefatory clause does not limit or expand the scope of the operative clause. . . . The prefatory clause does not suggest that preserving the militia was the only reason Americans valued the ancient right; most undoubtedly thought it even more important for self-defense and hunting." Turning to the operative clause—"to keep and bear Arms"—he added: "Although the phrase implies that the carrying of the weapon is for the purpose of 'offensive or defensive action,' it in no way connotes participation in a structured military organization. . . . [T]he most natural reading of 'keep Arms' in the Second Amendment is to have weapons." After separating those clauses, he focused on "the right of the people" and offered an intratextualist analysis, emphasizing that "in all six other provisions of the Constitution that mention 'the people,' the term unambiguously refers to all members of the political community, not an unspecified subset. . . . Putting all of these textual elements together, we find that they guarantee the individual right to possess and carry weapons in case of confrontation." Finally, Justice Scalia drew on the "original understanding" of the amendment, which he asserted applied "to weapons that were not specifically designed for military use and were not employed in a military capacity." "In sum," he concluded, "the District's ban on handgun possession in the home violates the Second Amendment, as does its prohibition against rendering any lawful firearm in the home operable for the purpose of immediate self-defense. Assuming that Heller is not disqualified from the exercise of Second Amendment rights, the District must permit him to register his handgun and must issue him a license to carry it in the home."

Justice Scalia's opinion for the Court, joined by Chief Justice Roberts and Justices Kennedy, Thomas, and Alito, however, emphasized that "the right secured by the Second Amendment is not unlimited." More specifically, Justice Scalia expressly emphasized that the amendment applies only to federal regulations and does not apply to the states under the Fourteenth Amendment. In underscoring that the decision applied only to the possession of handguns in one's home for purpose of self-defense, he noted that "we do not read the Second Amendment to protect the right of citizens to carry arms for any sort of confrontation, just as we do not read the First Amendment to protect the right of citizens to speak for any purpose." Justice Scalia also noted that the decision did not apply to other long-standing restrictions, such as prohibitions on the possession of firearms by felons and the mentally ill, the carrying of concealed weapons, as well as to bans on the carrying of firearms into schools and government buildings, and to conditions imposed on the commercial sale of firearms. In addition, he emphasized the narrowness of the ruling as applying only to "the sorts of weapons protected . . . 'in common use at the time'" of the ratification of the amendment; thus, leaving open the regulation of semi-automatic, assault and other weapons.

Subsequently, without mentioning the Second Amendment or the ruling in Heller, the Court upheld a federal statute, as amended in 1996, banning the possession of firearms by individuals convicted of felonies or of "a misdemeanor of domestic violence." Justice Ginsburg wrote for the Court in United States v. Hayes, 129 S.Ct. 1079 (2009), and Chief Justice Roberts and Justice Scalia dissented.

5

FREEDOM OF EXPRESSION
AND ASSOCIATION

A | *Judicial Approaches to the First Amendment*

In *Pleasant Grove City v. Summum* (2009) (excerpted below) the Roberts Court further extended the doctrine that the First Amendment does not apply to *government-sponsored speech*. In reversing the appellate court, Justice Alito held that under the First Amendment Free Speech Clause a small religious sect, the Summum, could not compel a city to erect a statue in a public park that contained a monument inscribed with the Ten Commandments and several other public displays. In so holding the Court extended prior rulings on government speech; see, e.g., *Rust v. Sullivan*, 500 U.S. 173 (1991) (excerpted in Vol. 2, Ch. 5), and *Rosenberger v. Rector and Visitors of the University of Virginia*, 515 U.S. 819 (1995) (excerpted in Vol. 2, Ch. 6).

In its 2009-2010 term, the Roberts Court will consider the constitutionality of a 1999 federal statute, 18 U.S.C. Sec. 48, making it a crime to depict animal cruelty in interstate or foreign commerce for commercial gain, carrying a fine and five-year sentence. Under that statute, Robert Stevens was arrested, tried, and convicted of three counts of distributing videos of fighting pit bulls; he was sentenced to thirty-seven months in prison by a federal district court. The Court of Appeals for the Third Circuit, however, reversed, 533 F 3d 218 (3rd Cir., 2008), holding that the statute was not a reasonable "time, place, and manner" restriction, and the government failed to show a compelling governmental interest, since animal cruelty (a separate crime) does not necessarily result in depictions of animal cruelty. In addition, the appellate court ruled that the statute was not narrowly tailored and that depictions of animal cruelty did not fall within a category of constitutionally unprotected speech under the First Amendment. The government appealed that decision and the Supreme Court granted review in *United States v. Stevens* (No. 08–769).

Pleasant Grove City v. Summum
129 S.Ct. 1125 (2009)

Pioneer Park is a two-and-a-half acre public park located in Pleasant Grove City, Utah. The park contains fifteen permanent displays, of which eleven were donated by private groups or individuals. They include an historic granary, a wishing well, the city's first fire station, a September 11, 2001 monument, and a Ten Commandments monument donated by the Fraternal Order of Eagles in 1971. Summum, a religious organization founded in 1975 and headquartered in Salt Lake City, requested permission to erect a "stone monument," which would contain "the Seven Aphorisms of SUMMUM," such as "Summum is mind, thought; the universe is a mental creation." The city denied the requests and explained that its practice was to limit monuments in the Park to those that "either (1) directly relate to the history of Pleasant Grove, or (2) were donated by groups with longstanding ties to the Pleasant Grove community." Subsequently, the city passed a resolution putting this policy into writing. The resolution also mentioned other criteria, such as safety and esthetics.

In 2005, Summum sued the city, asserting that it violated the Free Speech Clause of the First Amendment by accepting the Ten Commandments monument but rejecting the proposed Seven Aphorisms monument. After a federal district court denied Summum's preliminary injunction request, Summum appealed and a panel of the Tenth Circuit reversed. The panel noted that it had previously found the Ten Commandments monument to be private rather than government speech and held that public parks have traditionally been regarded as public forums; thus, the city could not reject the Seven Aphorisms monument unless it had a compelling justification.

The appellate court's decision was reversed. Justice Alito delivered the opinion for the Court. Justices Stevens, Breyer, Souter, and Scalia each filed concurring opinions.

☐ *JUSTICE ALITO delivered the opinion of the Court.*

No prior decision of this Court has addressed the application of the Free Speech Clause to a government entity's acceptance of privately donated, permanent monuments for installation in a public park, and the parties disagree sharply about the line of precedents that governs this situation. . . .

If petitioners were engaging in their own expressive conduct, then the Free Speech Clause has no application. The Free Speech Clause restricts government regulation of private speech; it does not regulate government speech. See *Johanns v. Livestock Marketing Assn.*, 544 U.S. 550 (2005). A government entity has the right to "speak for itself." *Board of Regents of Univ. of Wis. System v. Southworth*, 529 U.S. 217 (2000). "[I]t is entitled to say what it wishes," *Rosenberger v. Rector and Visitors of Univ. of Va.*, 515 U.S. 819 (1995), and to select the views that it wants to express. See *Rust v. Sullivan*, 500 U.S. 173 (1991).

Indeed, it is not easy to imagine how government could function if it lacked this freedom. "If every citizen were to have a right to insist that no one paid by public funds express a view with which he disagreed, debate over issues of great concern to the public would be limited to those in the private sector, and the process of government as we know it radically transformed." *Keller v. State Bar of Cal.*, 496 U.S. 1 (1990).

A government entity may exercise this same freedom to express its views when it receives assistance from private sources for the purpose of delivering a government-controlled message.

This does not mean that there are no restraints on government speech. For example, government speech must comport with the Establishment Clause. The involvement of public officials in advocacy may be limited by law, regulation, or practice. And of course, a government entity is ultimately "accountable to the electorate and the political process for its advocacy." "If the citizenry objects, newly elected officials later could espouse some different or contrary position."

While government speech is not restricted by the Free Speech Clause, the government does not have a free hand to regulate private speech on government property. This Court long ago recognized that members of the public retain strong free speech rights when they venture into public streets and parks, "which 'have immemorially been held in trust for the use of the public and, time out of mind, have been used for purposes of assembly, communicating thoughts between citizens, and discussing public questions.'" *Perry Ed. Assn. v. Perry Local Educators' Assn.*, 460 U.S. 37 (1983)(quoting *Hague v. Committee for Industrial Organization*, 307 U.S. 496 (1939). In order to preserve this freedom, government entities are strictly limited in their ability to regulate private speech in such "traditional public fora." Reasonable time, place, and manner restrictions are allowed, but any restriction based on the content of the speech must satisfy strict scrutiny, that is, the restriction must be narrowly tailored to serve a compelling government interest, and restrictions based on viewpoint are prohibited.

With the concept of the traditional public forum as a starting point, this Court has recognized that members of the public have free speech rights on other types of government property and in certain other government programs that share essential attributes of a traditional public forum. We have held that a government entity may create "a designated public forum" if government property that has not traditionally been regarded as a public forum is intentionally opened up for that purpose. Government restrictions on speech in a designated public forum are subject to the same strict scrutiny as restrictions in a traditional public forum. The Court has also held that a government entity may create a forum that is limited to use by certain groups or dedicated solely to the discussion of certain subjects. In such a forum, a government entity may impose restrictions on speech that are reasonable and viewpoint-neutral.

There may be situations in which it is difficult to tell whether a government entity is speaking on its own behalf or is providing a forum for private speech, but this case does not present such a situation. Permanent monuments displayed on public property typically represent government speech.

Governments have long used monuments to speak to the public. Since ancient times, kings, emperors, and other rulers have erected statues of themselves to remind their subjects of their authority and power. Triumphal arches, columns, and other monuments have been built to commemorate military victories and sacrifices and other events of civic importance. A monument, by definition, is a structure that is designed as a means of expression. When a government entity arranges for the construction of a monument, it does so because it wishes to convey some thought or instill some feeling in those who see the structure. . . .

Just as government-commissioned and government-financed monuments speak for the government, so do privately financed and donated monuments that the government accepts and displays to the public on government land. It certainly is not common for property owners to open up their property for the installation of permanent monuments that convey a message with which they do not wish to be associated. And because property owners typically do not permit the construction of such monuments on their land, persons who observe donated monuments routinely—and reasonably—interpret them as conveying some message on the property owner's behalf. In this context, there is little chance that observers will fail to appreciate the identity of the speaker. This is true whether the monument is located on private property or on public property, such as national, state, or city park land. . . .

But while government entities regularly accept privately funded or donated monuments, they have exercised selectivity. An example discussed by the city of New York as *amicus curiae* is illustrative. In the wake of the controversy generated in 1876 when the city turned down a donated monument to honor Daniel Webster, the city adopted rules governing the acceptance of artwork for permanent placement in city parks, requiring, among other things, that "any proposed gift of art had to be viewed either in its finished condition or as a model before acceptance." Across the country, "municipalities generally exercise editorial control over donated monuments through prior submission requirements, design input, requested modifications, written criteria, and legislative approvals of specific content proposals." . . .

In this case, it is clear that the monuments in Pleasant Grove's Pioneer Park represent government speech. Although many of the monuments were not designed or built by the City and were donated in completed form by private entities, the City decided to accept those donations and to display them in the Park. Respondent does not claim that the City ever opened up the Park for the placement of whatever permanent monuments might be offered by private donors. Rather, the City has "effectively controlled" the messages sent by the monuments in the Park by exercising "final approval authority" over their selection. The City has selected those monuments that it wants to display for the purpose of presenting the image of the City that it wishes to project to all who frequent the Park; it has taken ownership of most of the monuments in the Park, including the Ten Commandments monument that is the focus of respondent's concern; and the City has now expressly set forth the criteria it will use in making future selections. . . .

Respondent seems to think that a monument can convey only one "message"—which is, presumably, the message intended by the donor—and that, if a government entity that accepts a monument for placement on its property does not formally embrace that message, then the government has not engaged in expressive conduct.

This argument fundamentally misunderstands the way monuments convey meaning. The meaning conveyed by a monument is generally not a simple one like " 'Beef. It's What's for Dinner.' " Even when a monument features the written word, the monument may be intended to be interpreted, and may in fact be interpreted by different observers, in a variety of ways. Monuments called to our attention by the briefing in this case illustrate this phenomenon.

What, for example, is "the message" of the Greco-Roman mosaic of the word "Imagine" that was donated to New York City's Central Park in memory of John Lennon? Some observers may "imagine" the musical contributions that John Lennon would have made if he had not been killed. Others may think of the lyrics of the Lennon song that obviously inspired the mosaic and may "imagine" a world without religion, countries, possessions, greed, or hunger. . . .

Contrary to respondent's apparent belief, it frequently is not possible to identify a single "message" that is conveyed by an object or structure, and consequently, the thoughts or sentiments expressed by a government entity that accepts and displays such an object may be quite different from those of either its creator or its donor. By accepting a privately donated monument and placing it on city property, a city engages in expressive conduct, but the intended and perceived significance of that conduct may not coincide with the thinking of the monument's donor or creator. Indeed, when a privately donated memorial is funded by many small donations, the donors themselves may differ in their interpretation of the monument's significance. By accepting such a monument, a government entity does not necessarily endorse the specific meaning that any particular donor sees in the monument.

The message that a government entity conveys by allowing a monument to remain on its property may also be altered by the subsequent addition of other monuments in the same vicinity. For example, following controversy over the original design of the Vietnam Veterans Memorial, a compromise was reached that called for the nearby addition of a flagstaff and bronze Three Soldiers statue, which many believed changed the overall effect of the memorial. . . .

A striking example of how the interpretation of a monument can evolve is provided by one of the most famous and beloved public monuments in the United States, the Statue of Liberty. The statue was given to this country by the Third French Republic to express republican solidarity and friendship between the two countries. . . . Only later did the statue come to be viewed as a beacon welcoming immigrants to a land of freedom.

[P]ublic parks can accommodate only a limited number of permanent monuments. Public parks have been used, " 'time out of mind, . . . for purposes of assembly, communicating thoughts between citizens, and discussing public questions,' " but "one would be hard pressed to find a 'long tradition' of allowing people to permanently occupy public space with any manner of monuments."

Speakers, no matter how long-winded, eventually come to the end of their remarks; persons distributing leaflets and carrying signs at some point tire and go home; monuments, however, endure. They monopolize the use of the land on which they stand and interfere permanently with other uses of public space. A public park, over the years, can provide a soapbox for a very large number of orators—often, for all who want to speak—but it is hard to imagine how a public park could be opened up for the installation of permanent monuments by every person or group wishing to engage in that form of expression. . . .

In sum, we hold that the City's decision to accept certain privately donated monuments while rejecting respondent's is best viewed as a form of government speech. As a result, the City's decision is not subject to the Free Speech Clause, and the Court of Appeals erred in holding otherwise. We therefore reverse.

☐ *JUSTICE STEVENS with whom Justice GINSBURG joins, concurring.*

This case involves a property owner's rejection of an offer to place a permanent display on its land. While I join the Court's persuasive opinion, I think the reasons justifying the city's refusal would have been equally valid if its acceptance of the monument, instead of being characterized as "government speech," had merely been deemed an implicit endorsement of the donor's message. . . .

☐ *JUSTICE BREYER, concurring.*

I agree with the Court and join its opinion. I do so, however, on the understanding that the "government speech" doctrine is a rule of thumb, not a rigid category. Were the City to discriminate in the selection of permanent monuments on grounds unrelated to the display's theme, say solely on political grounds, its action might well violate the First Amendment. In my view, courts must apply categories such as "government speech," "public forums," "limited public forums," and "nonpublic forums" with an eye towards their purposes—lest we turn "free speech" doctrine into a jurisprudence of labels. Consequently, we must sometimes look beyond an initial categorization. And, in doing so, it helps to ask whether a government action burdens speech disproportionately in light of the action's tendency to further a legitimate government objective[.] Were we to do so here, we would find—for reasons that the Court sets forth—that the City's action, while preventing Summum from erecting its monument, does not disproportionately restrict Summum's freedom of expression. After all, parks do not serve speech-related interests alone. To the contrary, cities use park space to further a variety of recreational, historical, educational, aesthetic, and other civic interests. To reserve to the City the power to pick and choose among proposed monuments according to criteria reasonably related to one or more of these legitimate ends restricts Summum's expression, but, given the impracticality of alternatives and viewed in light of the City's legitimate needs, the restriction is not disproportionate. Analyzed either way, as "government speech" or as a proportionate restriction on Summum's expression, the City's action here is lawful.

☐ *JUSTICE SOUTER, concurring in the judgment.*

I agree with the Court that the Ten Commandments monument is government speech, that is, an expression of a government's position on the moral and religious issues raised by the subject of the monument. I have qualms, however, about accepting the position that public monuments are government speech categorically.

Because the government speech doctrine, as Justice Stevens notes, is "recently minted," it would do well for us to go slow in setting its bounds, which will affect existing doctrine in ways not yet explored. Even though, for example, Establishment Clause issues have been neither raised nor briefed before us, there is no doubt that this case and its government speech claim has been litigated by the parties with one eye on the Establishment Clause. The interaction between the "government speech doctrine" and Establishment Clause principles has not, however, begun to be worked out.

The case shows that it may not be easy to work out. After today's decision, whenever a government maintains a monument it will presumably be understood to be engaging in government speech. If the monument has some religious character, the specter of violating the Establishment Clause will behoove it to take care to avoid the appearance of a flat-out establishment of religion, in the sense of the government's adoption of the tenets expressed or symbolized. In such an instance, there will be safety in numbers, and it will be in the interest of a careful government to accept other monuments to stand nearby, to dilute the appearance of adopting whatever particular religious position the single example alone might stand for. As mementoes and testimonials pile up, however, the chatter may well make it less intuitively obvious that the government is speaking in its own right simply by maintaining the monuments. . . .

☐ *JUSTICE SCALIA with whom Justice THOMAS joins, concurring.*

As framed and argued by the parties, this case presents a question under the Free Speech Clause of the First Amendment. I agree with the Court's analysis of that question and join its opinion in full. But it is also obvious that from the start, the case has been litigated in the shadow of the First Amendment's Establishment Clause . . . .

The city ought not fear that today's victory has propelled it from the Free Speech Clause frying pan into the Establishment Clause fire. Contrary to respondent's intimations, there are very good reasons to be confident that the park displays do not violate any part of the First Amendment.

In *Van Orden v. Perry*, 545 U.S. 677 (2005), this Court upheld against Establishment Clause challenge a virtually identical Ten Commandments monument, donated by the very same organization (the Fraternal Order of Eagles), which was displayed on the grounds surrounding the Texas State Capitol. Nothing in that decision suggested that the outcome turned on a finding that the monument was only "private" speech. To the contrary, all the Justices agreed that government speech was at issue, but the Establishment Clause argument was nonetheless rejected. For the plurality, that was because the Ten Commandments "have an undeniable historical meaning" in addition to their "religious significance." Justice Breyer, concurring in the judgment, agreed that the monument conveyed a permissible secular message, as evidenced by its location in a park that contained multiple monuments and historical markers; by the fact that it had been donated by the Eagles "as part of that organization's efforts to combat juvenile delinquency"; and by the length of time (40 years) for which the monument had gone unchallenged.

Even accepting the narrowest reading of the narrowest opinion necessary to the judgment in *Van Orden*, there is little basis to distinguish the monument in this case: Pioneer Park includes "15 permanent displays;" it was donated by the Eagles as part of its national effort to combat juvenile delinquency; and it was erected in 1971, which means it is approaching its (momentous!) 40th anniversary.

The city can safely exhale. Its residents and visitors can now return to enjoying Pioneer Park's wishing well, its historic granary—and, yes, even its Ten Commandments monument—without fear that they are complicit in an establishment of religion.

B | *Obscenity, Pornography, and Offensive Speech*

In its 2007–2008 term the Court upheld the so-called PROTECT Act of 2003 aimed at curbing the pandering and proliferation of child pornography on the Internet. The law makes it a federal crime for any person who "knowingly . . . advertises, promotes, distributes, or solicits . . . any material or purported material in a manner that reflects the belief, or that is intended to cause another to believe, that the material or purported material is, or contains – (i) an obscene visual depiction of a minor engaging in sexually explicit conduct; or (ii) a visual depiction of an actual minor engaging in sexually explicit conduct." In doing so, the majority extended its earlier rulings on permitting the prosecution of pandering allegedly obscene materials (as discussed in Vol. 2, Ch. 5), but departed from its more recent decisions extending First Amendment protection to the Internet. Writing for the Court, Justice Scalia held that the law was neither overly broad in violation of the First Amendment nor unconstitutionally vague under the due process clause. Justice Souter, joined by Justice Ginsburg, dissented, arguing that the law swept too broadly in covering artistic works, such as *Romeo and Juliet*, and "virtual child pornography," which the Court ruled the First Amendment protects in *Ashcroft v. Free Speech Coalition*, 534 U.S. 234 (2002) (excerpted in Vol. 2, Ch. 5). The Court's ruling in *United States v. Williams* (2008) is excerpted below in Section F.

F | *Regulating the Broadcast and Cable Media, and the Internet*

By a seven-to-two vote in *United States v. Williams* (2008) (excerpted below), the Court upheld the so-called PROTECT Act of 2003 aimed at curbing the pandering and proliferation of child pornography on the Internet. The law makes it a federal crime for any person who "knowingly . . . advertises, promotes, distributes, or solicits . . . any material or purported material in a manner that reflects the belief, or that is intended to cause another to believe, that the material or purported material is, or contains – (i) an obscene visual depiction of a minor engaging in sexually explicit conduct; or (ii) a visual depiction of an actual minor engaging in sexually explicit conduct." Writing for the Court, Justice Scalia held that the law was neither overly broad in violation of the First Amendment nor unconstitutionally vague under the due process clause. Justice Souter, joined by Justice Ginsburg, dissented, arguing that the law swept too broadly in covering artistic works, such as *Romeo and Juliet*, and "virtual child pornography," which the Court ruled the First Amendment protects in *Ashcroft v. Free Speech Coalition*, 534 U.S. 234 (2002) (excerpted in Vol. 2, Ch. 5).

In its 2008–2009 term, the Roberts Court reconsidered challenges to the Federal Communications Commission's enforcement of "indecency" standards in *Federal Communications Commission v. Fox Television Stations*. The Court last considered the matter thirty years ago, in *Federal Communications Commission v. Pacifica Foundation*, 438 U.S. 726 (1978) (excerpted in Vol. 2, Ch. 5), when it upheld the FCC's "indecency" standards in ruling on the satirist George Carlin's twelve-minute monologue on the "seven dirty words" that can't be said on the airwaves. The lawsuit in *Federal Communications Commission v. Fox Television Stations*, 129 S.Ct. 1800 (2009) was brought after the FCC reprimanded Fox Television for airing brief expletives of singer Cher in 2002 and Nicole Richie in 2003 at the Billboards Music Awards. In 2004, after Janet Jackson's "wardrobe malfunction" during a Super Bowl performance led to a $550,000 fine against CBS television stations, the FCC adopted the position that even brief, "fleeting" expletives expose networks to sanctions because new technology makes it easier to censor such "indecency." By contrast, Fox and other networks argued that the FCC exceeded its authority when an expletive does not convey a sexual message. The Court of Appeals for Second Circuit agreed that the FCC's policy was "arbitrary and capricious" under the Administrative Procedure Act and the First Amendment. But the Roberts Court reversed the appellate court's decision. Writing for the majority, Justice Scalia upheld the FCC's change in policy on indecent broadcasts under the Administrative Procedure Act, holding that it was not "arbitrary" or "capricious" in sanctioning the broadcasting of fleeting expletives. Notably, though, the Court declined to rule on the constitutionality of the FCC's policy under the First Amendment. Justices Kennedy and Thomas filed concurring opinions. Justices Stevens, Ginsburg, and Breyer filed dissenting opinions; Justice Souter joined the latter's dissent. Dissenting Justice Stevens, who delivered the opinion in *Pacifica Foundation*, sharply criticized the majority for "assuming that *Pacifica* endorsed a construction of the term 'indecent' that would include any expletive that has a sexual or excretory origin. ... Our holding was narrow in two critical respects.

First, we concluded . . . that the statutory term 'indecent' was not limited to material that had prurient appeal and instead included material that was in 'nonconformance with accepted standards of morality.' Second, we upheld the FCC's adjudication that a 12-minute, expletive-filled monologue by satiric humorist George Carlin was indecent 'as broadcast.' We did not decide whether an isolated expletive could qualify as indecent. And we certainly did not hold that any word with a sexual or scatological origin, however used, was indecent." Justice Stevens also emphasized that:

> There is a critical distinction between the use of an expletive to describe a sexual or excretory function and the use of such a word for an entirely different purpose, such as to express an emotion. One rests at the core of indecency; the other stands miles apart. As any golfer who has watched his partner shank a short approach knows, it would be absurd to accept the suggestion that the resultant four-letter word uttered on the golf course describes sex or excrement and is therefore indecent.

United States v. Williams
128 S.Ct. 1830 (2008)

In response to the Court's ruling in *Ashcroft v. Free Speech Coalition*, 534 U.S. 234 (2002) (excerpted in Vol. 2, Ch. 5), which struck down provisions of the Child Pornography Prevention Act of 1996 that made it a crime to distribute or possess "virtual child pornography," Congress enacted the Prosecutorial Remedies and Other Tools to end the Exploitation of Children Today Act of 2003 (the PROTECT Act). Part of that law, Section 2252(a)(3)(B), makes it a federal crime for any person who "knowingly . . . advertises, promotes, or solicits . . . any material or purported material in a manner that reflects the belief, or that is intended to cause another to believe, that the material or purported material is, or contains − (i) an obscene visual depiction of a minor engaging in sexually explicit conduct; or (ii) a visual depiction of an actual minor engaging in sexually explicit conduct." Subsequently, in 2004 Michael Williams, using a sexually explicit screen name, signed into an Internet chat room. A Secret Service agent had also signed into the chat room under the moniker "Lisa n Miami." The agent noticed that Williams had posted a message that read: "Dad of toddler has 'good' pics of her an [sic] me for swap of your toddler pics, or live cam." The agent struck up a conversation with Williams, leading to an electronic exchange of non-pornographic pictures of children. Later, Williams messaged that he had photographs of men molesting his four-year-old daughter. Suspicious that "Lisa n Miami" was a law-enforcement agent, before proceeding further Williams demanded that the agent produce additional pictures. When he did not, Williams posted the following public message in the chat room: "HERE ROOM; I CAN PUT UPLINK CUZ IM FOR REAL—SHE CANT." Appended to this declaration was a hyperlink that led to seven pictures of actual children, aged approximately five to fifteen, engaging in sexually explicit conduct and displaying their genitals. The Secret Service then obtained a search warrant for Williams's home, where agents seized two hard drives containing twenty-two images of real children engaged in sexually explicit conduct. Williams was charged with one count of pandering child pornography under Section 2252A (a)(3)(B) and one count of possessing child pornography under Section 2252A(a)(5)(B). He pleaded guilty to both counts but reserved the right to challenge the constitutionality of the pandering conviction. The District Court rejected his challenge and sentenced him to concurrent sixty-month sentences. The Court of Appeals for the Eleventh Circuit reversed the pandering conviction, holding that the statute was both overbroad and impermissibly vague. In its view, the statute was broad enough to include any "braggart, exaggerator, or outright liar" who claimed to have child pornography. The government appealed and the Supreme Court granted *certiorari*.

The appellate court's decision was reversed by a seven-to-two vote. Justice Scalia delivered the opinion of the Court. Justice Stevens filed a concurring opinion, while Justice Souter, joined by Justice Ginsburg, issued a dissenting opinion.

□ *JUSTICE SCALIA delivered the opinion of the Court.*

Section 2252A(a)(3)(B) of Title 18, United States Code, criminalizes, in certain specified circumstances, the pandering or solicitation of child pornography. This case presents the question whether that statute is overbroad under the First Amendment or impermissibly vague under the Due Process Clause of the Fifth Amendment.

We have long held that obscene speech—sexually explicit material that violates fundamental notions of decency—is not protected by the First Amendment. See *Roth v. United States*, 354 U.S. 476 (1957). But to protect explicit material that has social value, we have limited the scope of the obscenity exception, and have overturned convictions for the distribution of sexually graphic but nonobscene material. See *Miller v. California*, 413 U.S. 15 (1973); see also, e.g., *Jenkins v. Georgia*, 418 U.S. 153 (1974).

Over the last 25 years, we have confronted a related and overlapping category of proscribable speech: child pornography. See *Ashcroft v. Free Speech Coalition*, 535 U.S. 234 (2002); *New York v. Ferber*, 458 U.S. 747 (1982). This consists of sexually explicit visual portrayals that feature children. We have held that a statute which proscribes the distribution of all child pornography, even material that does not qualify as obscenity, does not on its face violate the First Amendment. Moreover, we have held that the government may criminalize the possession of child pornography, even though it may not criminalize the mere possession of obscene material involving adults.

The broad authority to proscribe child pornography is not, however, unlimited. Four Terms ago, we held facially overbroad two provisions of the federal Child Pornography Protection Act of 1996 (CPPA). *Free Speech Coalition.* The first of these banned the possession and distribution of "'any visual depiction'" that "'is, or appears to be, of a minor engaging in sexually explicit conduct,'" even if it contained only youthful-looking adult actors or virtual images of children generated by a computer. This was invalid, we explained, because the child-protection rationale for speech restriction does not apply to materials produced without children. The second provision at issue in *Free Speech Coalition* criminalized the possession and distribution of material that had been pandered as child pornography, regardless of whether it actually was that. A person could thus face prosecution for possessing unobjectionable material that someone else had pandered. We held that this prohibition, which did "more than prohibit pandering," was also facially overbroad.

After our decision in *Free Speech Coalition*, Congress went back to the drawing board and produced legislation with the unlikely title of the Prosecutorial Remedies and Other Tools to end the Exploitation of Children Today Act of 2003. We shall refer to it as the Act. Section 503 of the Act amended 18 U.S.C. Section 2252A to add a new pandering and solicitation provision, relevant portions of which now read as follows:

"(a) Any person who—
"(3)knowingly—
"(B)advertises, promotes, presents, distributes, or solicits through the mails, or in interstate or foreign commerce by any means, including by computer, any material or purported material in a manner that reflects the belief, or that is intended to cause another to believe, that the material or purported material is, or contains—
"(i)an obscene visual depiction of a minor engaging in sexually explicit conduct; or
"(ii) a visual depiction of an actual minor engaging in sexually explicit conduct, "shall be punished as provided in subsection (b)."

Section 2256(2)(A) defines "sexually explicit conduct" as "actual or simulated—

"(i)sexual intercourse, including genital-genital, oral-genital, anal-genital, or oral-anal, whether between persons of the same or opposite sex;
"(ii)bestiality;
"(iii)masturbation;
"(iv)sadistic or masochistic abuse; or
"(v)lascivious exhibition of the genitals or pubic area of any person."

Violation of Section 2252A(a)(3)(B) incurs a minimum sentence of five years' imprisonment and a maximum of twenty years.

The Act's express findings indicate that Congress was concerned that limiting the child-pornography prohibition to material that could be proved to feature actual children, as our decision in *Free Speech Coalition* required, would enable many child pornographers to evade conviction. The emergence of new technology and the repeated retransmission of picture files over the Internet could make it nearly impossible to prove that a particular image was produced using real children—even though "[t]here is no substantial evidence that any of the child pornography images being trafficked today were made other than by the abuse of real children," virtual imaging being prohibitively expensive. . . .

According to our First Amendment overbreadth doctrine, a statute is facially invalid if it prohibits a substantial amount of protected speech. The doctrine seeks to strike a balance between competing social costs. *Virginia v. Hicks*, 539 U.S. 113 (2003). On the one hand, the threat of enforcement of an overbroad law deters people from engaging in constitutionally protected speech, inhibiting the free exchange of ideas. On the other hand, invalidating a law that in some of its applications is perfectly constitutional—particularly a law directed at conduct so antisocial that it has been made criminal—has obvious harmful effects. In order to maintain an appropriate balance, we have vigorously enforced the requirement that a statute's overbreadth be substantial, not only in an absolute sense, but also relative to the statute's plainly legitimate sweep.

The first step in overbreadth analysis is to construe the challenged statute; it is impossible to determine whether a statute reaches too far without first knowing what the statute covers. Generally speaking, Section 2252A(a)(3)(B) prohibits offers to provide and requests to obtain child pornography. The statute does not require the actual existence of child pornography. In this respect, it differs from the statutes in *Ferber*, and *Free Speech Coalition*, which prohibited the possession or distribution of child pornography. Rather than targeting the underlying material, this statute bans the collateral speech that introduces such material into the child-pornography distribution network. Thus, an Internet user who solicits child pornography from an undercover agent violates the statute, even if the officer possesses no child pornography. Likewise, a person who advertises virtual child pornography as depicting actual children also falls within the reach of the statute.

The statute's definition of the material or purported material that may not be pandered or solicited precisely tracks the material held constitutionally proscribable in *Ferber* and *Miller*: obscene material depicting (actual or virtual) children engaged in sexually explicit conduct, and any other material depicting actual children engaged in sexually explicit conduct. . . .

We now turn to whether the statute, as we have construed it, criminalizes a substantial amount of protected expressive activity.

Offers to engage in illegal transactions are categorically excluded from First Amendment protection. *Pittsburgh Press Co. v. Pittsburgh Comm'n on Human Relations*, 413 U.S. 376 (1973). One would think that this principle resolves the present case, since the statute criminalizes only offers to provide or requests to obtain contraband—child obscenity and child pornography involving actual children, both of which are proscribed, and the proscription of which is constitutional. The Eleventh Circuit, however, believed that the exclusion of First Amendment protection extended only to commercial offers to provide or receive contraband.

This mistakes the rationale for the categorical exclusion. It is based not on the less privileged First Amendment status of commercial speech, see *Central Hudson Gas & Elec. Corp. v. Public Serv. Comm'n of N.Y.*, 447 U.S. 557 (1980), but on the principle that offers to give or receive what it is unlawful to possess have no social value and thus, like obscenity, enjoy no First Amendment protection. Many long established criminal proscriptions—such as laws against conspiracy, incitement, and solicitation—criminalize speech (commercial or not) that is intended to induce or commence illegal activities. Offers to provide or requests to obtain unlawful material, whether as part of a commercial exchange or not, are similarly undeserving of First Amendment protection. It would be an odd constitutional principle that permitted the government to prohibit offers to sell illegal drugs, but not offers to give them away for free. . . .

In sum, we hold that offers to provide or requests to obtain child pornography are categorically excluded from the First Amendment. . . .

Child pornography harms and debases the most defenseless of our citizens. Both the State and Federal Governments have sought to suppress it for many years, only to find it proliferating through the new medium of the Internet. This Court held unconstitutional Congress's previous attempt to meet this new threat, and Congress responded with a carefully crafted attempt to eliminate the First Amendment problems we identified. As far as the provision at issue in this case is concerned, that effort was successful.

The judgment of the Eleventh Circuit is reversed.

□ *JUSTICE STEVENS, with whom Justice BREYER joins, concurring.*

My conclusion that this statutory provision is not facially unconstitutional is buttressed by two interrelated considerations on which Justice SCALIA finds it unnecessary to rely. First, I believe the result to be compelled by the principle that "every reasonable construction must be resorted to, in order to save a statute from unconstitutionality," *Hooper v. California*, 155 U.S. 648 (1895).

Second, to the extent the statutory text alone is unclear, our duty to avoid constitutional objections makes it especially appropriate to look beyond the text in order to ascertain the intent of its drafters. It is abundantly clear from the provision's legislative history that Congress' aim was to target materials advertised, promoted, presented, distributed, or solicited with a lascivious purpose—that is, with the intention of inciting sexual arousal. The provision was described throughout the deliberations in both Houses of Congress as the "pandering," or "pandering and solicitation" provision, despite the fact that the term "pandering" appears nowhere in the statute. . . .

The dissent argues that the statute impermissibly undermines our First Amendment precedents insofar as it covers proposals to transact in constitutionally protected material. It is true that proof that a pornographic but not obscene representation did not depict real children would place that representation on the protected side of the line. But any constitutional concerns that might arise on that score are surely answered by the construction the Court gives the statute's operative provisions; that is, proposing a transaction in such material would not give rise to criminal liability under the statute unless the defendant actually believed, or intended to induce another to believe, that the material in question depicted real children.

Accordingly, when material which is protected—particularly if it possesses serious literary, artistic, political, or scientific value—is advertised, promoted, presented, distributed, or solicited for some lawful and nonlascivious purpose, such conduct is not captured by the statutory prohibition.

☐ *Justice SOUTER, with whom Justice GINSBURG joins, dissenting.*

Dealing in obscenity is penalized without violating the First Amendment, but as a general matter pornography lacks the harm to justify prohibiting it. If, however, a photograph (to take the kind of image in this case) shows an actual minor child as a pornographic subject, its transfer and even its possession may be made criminal. *New York v. Ferber,* 458 U.S. 747 (1982). The exception to the general rule rests not on the content of the picture but on the need to foil the exploitation of child subjects, and the justification limits the exception: only pornographic photographs of actual children may be prohibited, see *Ashcroft v. Free Speech Coalition,* 535 U.S. 234(2002). Thus, just six years ago the Court struck down a statute outlawing particular material merely represented to be child pornography, but not necessarily depicting actual children.

The Prosecutorial Remedies and Other Tools to end the Exploitation of Children Today Act of 2003 (Act) was enacted in the wake of *Free Speech Coalition.* The Act responds by avoiding any direct prohibition of transactions in child pornography when no actual minors may be pictured; instead, it prohibits proposals for transactions in pornography when a defendant manifestly believes or would induce belief in a prospective party that the subject of an exchange or exhibition is or will be an actual child, not an impersonated, simulated or "virtual" one, or the subject of a composite created from lawful photos spliced together. The Act specifically prohibits three types of those proposals. It outlaws solicitation of child pornography, as well as two distinct kinds of offers: those "advertis[ing]" or "promot[ing]" prosecutable child pornography, which recommend the material with the implication that the speaker can make it available, and those "present[ing]" or "distribut[ing]" such child pornography, which make the material available to anyone who chooses to take it.

The Court holds it is constitutional to prohibit these proposals, and up to a point I do not disagree. In particular, I accept the Court's explanation that Congress may criminalize proposals unrelated to any extant image. I part ways from the Court, however, on the regulation of proposals made with regard to specific, existing representations. Under the new law, the elements of the pandering offense are the same, whether or not the images are of real children. As to those that do not show real children, of course, a transaction in the material could not be prosecuted consistently with the First Amendment, and I believe that maintaining the First Amendment protection of expression we have previously held to cover fake child pornography requires a limit to the law's criminalization of pandering proposals. In failing to confront the tension between ostensibly protecting the material pandered while approving prosecution of the pandering of that same material, and in allowing the new pandering prohibition to suppress otherwise protected speech, the Court undermines *Ferber* and *Free Speech Coalition* in both reasoning and result. This is the significant element of today's holding, and I respectfully dissent from it. . . .

H | *Symbolic Speech and Speech-Plus-Conduct*

■ THE DEVELOPMENT OF LAW

Places That Have Been Held Not to Be Public Forums

CASE	VOTE	RULING
Pleasant Grove City v. Summum, 129 S.Ct. 1446 (2009)		Unlike speech in a public park or other public forum, the Court held that a city's decision about

what kinds of permanent monuments to permit constituted *government speech*, and thus the public forum doctrine does not apply. (The case is excerpted in this chapter.)

6

Freedom from and of Religion

A | The (Dis)Establishment of Religion

In its 2009–2010 term, the Roberts Court will revisit the controversy over the public display of religious displays in *Salazar v. Buono* (No. 08–472), involving whether an eight-foot cross in the Mojave National Preserve is an unconstitutional governmental endorsement of religion. Erected in 1934 by the Veterans of Foreign Wars, the cross has been maintained as a memorial by the National Park Service. The American Civil Liberties Union filed a suit in 2001 on behalf of a former park service officer, Frank Buono, a Catholic, who alleged that the cross violated the Establishment Clause of the First Amendment. The suit also noted that the Park Service had denied a request to have a Buddhist shrine erected near the cross. A federal district court agreed with Buono, ruling in 2002 that the "primary effect of the presence of the cross" was to "advance religion." Congress responded in 2004 by enacting legislation directing the Department of the Interior to transfer about an acre of land to the Veterans of Foreign Wars in exchange for a privately owned plot nearby. In 2007, a three-judge panel of the U.S. Court of Appeals for the Ninth Circuit upheld the lower court's decision and invalidated the land transfer, observing that "carving out a tiny parcel of property in the midst of this vast preserve—like a donut hole with the cross atop it—will do nothing to minimize the impermissible government endorsement" of a religious symbol. The Bush administration appealed that ruling to the Supreme Court, contending that the "seriously misguided decision" would require the government to "tear down a cross that has stood without incident for 70 years as a memorial to fallen service members." The government also questioned whether Buono had standing to sue, since he lives in Oregon and suffers no specific harm because of the cross. The questions presented are whether an individual has Article III standing to bring an Establishment Clause suit challenging the display of a religious symbol on government land, and whether an act of Congress directing the land to be transferred to a private entity was permissible under the First Amendment.

7

THE FOURTH AMENDMENT
GUARANTEE AGAINST
UNREASONABLE SEARCHES
AND SEIZURES

B | Exceptions to the Fourth Amendment Warrant Requirement

In *Arizona v. Johnson* 129 S.Ct. 781(2009), the Court further extended the "stop and frisk" exception to the Fourth Amendment laid down in *Terry v. Ohio*, 392 U.S. 1 (1968) (excerpted in Vol. 2, Ch. 7). In *Terry* the Court ruled that a "stop and frisk" may be conducted without violating the Fourth Amendment guarantee against unreasonable searches and seizures if (a) in an investigatory stop police have a reasonable suspicion that a person is committing or has committed a crime, and (b) police proceed from a stop to a pat-down search for weapons based on a reasonable suspicion the individual is armed and dangerous. Subsequent decisions expanded that exception with respect to traffic stops. In *Brendlin v. California*, 591 U.S. 249 (2007), for instance, the Court held that during a traffic stop police may seize "everyone in the vehicle"—the driver and all passengers. In *Arizona v. Johnson*, Justice Ginsburg held for a unanimous Court that police may order a passenger out of a stopped vehicle and conduct a pat-down search if they have reason to believe that the rider is armed and dangerous, and therefore poses a threat to police and the public.

Arizona v. Johnson stemmed from a police patrol of gang activity in a neighborhood associated with gangs in Tucson, Arizona. When one car passed, an officer ran a check on the license plate and found that insurance on the vehicle was suspended. Hence, although there was no suspicion of crime, the officers stopped the car to question the driver and one of the officers engaged a back-seat passenger, Lemon Montrea Johnson, who was wearing a blue bandanna—a gang emblem of the Crips. The officer learned from her conversation with Johnson that he was from town, he was associated with gang activity, and he had done time on a burglary conviction. Whereupon the officer ordered him out of the car, frisked him, and felt a gun near his waist. Johnson was arrested, tried, and convicted for illegal weapons possession. A state appellate court, however, reversed his conviction on the ground that police based the search only on their conversation with him, and on no reasonable suspicion that he had committed a crime. The Supreme Court reversed that decision.

In its 2008–2009 term, a bare majority of the Roberts Court limited warrantless car searches and reaffirmed the holding in *Chimel v. California*, 395 U.S. 752 (1969)(excerpted in Vol. 2, Ch. 7), as extended to automobiles in *New York v. Belton*, 453 U.S. 454 (1981), and in *Arizona v. Gant* (2009) (excerpted in Section C of this chapter).

C | The Special Problems of Automobiles in a Mobile Society

The Roberts Court ruled unanimously that police do not act unconstitutionally in conducting a search of a driver following an arrest based on probable cause, even if the arrest violates a state law. Delivering the decision in *Virginia v. Moore* (excerpted below), Justice Scalia upheld the conviction of David Moore for possession of crack cocaine after he was stopped for driving on a suspended license, which under state law authorized a traffic citation, not an arrest. As long as police have probable cause to make an arrest, Justice Scalia held, it makes no difference that a state law bars police from making an arrest when the crime involved is only a misdemeanor traffic offense. "An arrest based on probable cause serves interests that have long been seen as sufficient to justify the seizure" of evidence after an arrest. Justice Scalia noted that with its policy of ticketing after a traffic offense, "Virginia chooses to protect individual privacy and dignity more than the Fourth Amendment requires." But he ruled that choice does not make a resulting search invalid under the Fourth Amendment. "Moore would allow Virginia to accord enhanced protection only on pain of accompanying that protection with federal remedies for Fourth

Amendment violations, which often include the exclusionary rule. States unwilling to lose control over the remedy would have to abandon restrictions on arrest altogether. This is an odd consequence of a provision designed to protect against searches and seizures."

In its 2008–2009 term, the Court also considered whether police violated the Fourth Amendment, during a routine traffic stop, by conducting a pat-down search of a passenger, based on an articulable basis to believe the passenger might be armed and dangerous, but not probable cause to believe the passenger is committing or has committed a criminal offense. The case, *Arizona v. Johnson*, 129 S.Ct. 781 (2009) is further discussed in Section B of this chapter.

In its 2008–2009 term, the Roberts Court split five to four in limiting warrantless car searches. Writing for the Court, Justice Stevens reaffirmed the holding in *Chimel v. California*, 895 U.S. 752 (1969) (excerpted in Vol. 2, Ch. 7), as extended in *New York v. Belton*, 453 U.S. 454 (1981), that police may search only the immediate area in order to protect the safety of officers in a search-incident-to-arrest; the police must have a warrant to search a car after the driver or passenger is taken into custody and may conduct a warrantless search only for evidence related to the arrest. Justice Scalia cast the deciding vote and issued a concurring opinion. Chief Justice Roberts and Justices Thomas, Breyer, and Alito dissented in *Arizona v. Gant* (2009) (excerpted below).

Arizona v. Gant
129 S.Ct. 1710 (2009)

Arizona police went to the home of Rodney Gant in search of drugs and to arrest him for failing to appear in court for having a suspended driver's license. When they arrived Gant was not there, but while the police were still there Gant pulled into the driveway. While Gant was in the car, an officer shined a flashlight into the vehicle, but made no other contact with him until he stepped out of the car. He was then arrested for driving with a suspended license, handcuffed, and locked in the back of a patrol car. Afterward, police officers searched his car and discovered cocaine in the pocket of a jacket on the backseat. Because Gant could not have accessed his car to retrieve weapons or evidence at the time of the search, on appeal, the Arizona Supreme Court held that the search-incident-to-arrest exception to the Fourth Amendment's warrant requirement, as defined in *Chimel v. California*, 395 U.S. 752 (1969), and applied to vehicle searches in *New York v. Belton*, 453 U.S. 454 (1981), did not justify the search in this case. The state appealed and the Supreme Court granted review.

The state supreme court's decision was affirmed by a five-to-four vote. Justice Stevens delivered the opinion of the Court. Justice Scalia issued a concurring opinion. Justices Breyer and Alito filed dissenting opinions; the latter's was joined by Chief Justice Roberts and Justice Thomas.

☐ *Justice STEVENS delivered the opinion of the Court.*

Under *Chimel*, police may search-incident-to-arrest only the space within an arrestee's "'immediate control,'" meaning "the area from within which he might gain possession of a weapon or destructible evidence." The safety and evidentiary justifications underlying *Chimel's* reaching-distance rule determine *Belton's* scope. Accordingly, we hold that *Belton* does not authorize a vehicle search incident to a recent occupant's arrest after the arrestee has been secured and cannot access the interior of the vehicle. Consistent with the holding in *Thornton v. United States*, 541 U.S. 615 (2004), and following the suggestion in Justice SCALIA's opinion concurring in the judgment in that case, we also conclude that circumstances unique to the automobile context justify a search-incident-to-arrest when it is reasonable to believe that evidence of the offense of arrest might be found in the vehicle. . . .

Consistent with our precedent, our analysis begins, as it should in every case addressing the reasonableness of a warrantless search, with the basic rule that "searches conducted outside the judicial process, without prior approval by judge or magistrate, are per se unreasonable under the Fourth Amendment—subject only to a few specifically established and well-delineated exceptions." *Katz v. United States*, 389 U.S. 347 (1967). Among the exceptions to the warrant requirement is a search incident to a lawful arrest. The exception derives from interests in officer safety and evidence preservation that are typically implicated in arrest situations.

In *Chimel*, we held that a search-incident-to-arrest may only include "the arrestee's person and the area 'within his immediate control'—construing that phrase to mean the area from within which he might gain possession of a weapon or destructible evidence." That limitation, which continues to define the boundaries of the exception, ensures that the scope of a search-incident-to-arrest is commensurate with its purposes of protecting arresting officers and safeguarding any evidence of the offense of arrest that an arrestee might conceal or destroy. If there is no possibility that an arrestee could reach into the area that law enforcement officers seek to search, both justifications for the search-incident-to-arrest exception are absent and the rule does not apply.

In *Belton*, we considered *Chimel's* application to the automobile context. A lone police officer in that case stopped a speeding car in which Belton was one of four occupants. While asking for the driver's license and registration, the officer smelled burnt marijuana and observed an envelope on the car floor marked "Supergold"—a name he associated with marijuana. Thus having probable cause to believe the occupants had committed a drug offense, the officer ordered them out of the vehicle, placed them under arrest, and patted them down. Without handcuffing the arrestees, the officer "'split them up into four separate areas of the Thruway . . . so they would not be in physical touching area of each other'" and searched the vehicle, including the pocket of a jacket on the backseat, in which he found cocaine. . . .

[W]e held that when an officer lawfully arrests "the occupant of an automobile, he may, as a contemporaneous incident of that arrest, search the passenger compartment of the automobile" and any containers therein. That holding was based in large part on our assumption "that articles inside the relatively narrow compass of the passenger compartment of an automobile are in fact generally, even if not inevitably, within 'the area into which an arrestee might reach.' "

The Arizona Supreme Court read our decision in *Belton* as merely delineating "the proper scope of a search of the interior of an automobile" incident to an arrest. That is, when the passenger compartment is within an arrestee's reaching distance, *Belton* supplies the generalization that the entire compartment and any containers therein may be reached. On that view of *Belton*, the state court concluded that the search of Gant's car was unreasonable because Gant clearly could not have accessed his car at the time of the search. It also found that no other exception to the warrant requirement applied in this case.

Despite the textual and evidentiary support for the Arizona Supreme Court's reading of *Belton*, our opinion has been widely understood to allow a vehicle search incident to the arrest of a recent occupant even if there is no possibility the arrestee could gain access to the vehicle at the time of the search. This reading may be attributable to Justice BRENNAN's dissent in *Belton*, in which he characterized the Court's holding as resting on the "fiction . . . that the interior of a car is always within the immediate control of an arrestee who has recently been in the car." Under the majority's approach, he argued, "the result would presumably be the same even if [the officer] had handcuffed Belton and his companions in the patrol car" before conducting the search.

Since we decided *Belton*, Courts of Appeals have given different answers to the question whether a vehicle must be within an arrestee's reach to justify a vehicle search incident to arrest, but Justice BRENNAN's reading of the Court's opinion has predominated. . . .

Under this broad reading of *Belton*, a vehicle search would be authorized incident to every arrest of a recent occupant notwithstanding that in most cases the vehicle's passenger compartment will not be within the arrestee's reach at the time of the search. To read *Belton* as authorizing a vehicle search incident to every recent occupant's arrest would thus untether the rule from the justifications underlying the *Chimel* exception—a result clearly incompatible with our statement in *Belton* that it "in no way alters the fundamental principles established in the *Chimel* case regarding the basic scope of searches incident to lawful custodial arrests." Accordingly, we reject this reading of *Belton* and hold that the *Chimel* rationale authorizes police to search a vehicle incident to a recent occupant's arrest only when the arrestee is unsecured and within reaching distance of the passenger compartment at the time of the search.

Although it does not follow from *Chimel*, we also conclude that circumstances unique to the vehicle context justify a search incident to a lawful arrest when it is "reasonable to believe evidence relevant to the crime of arrest might be found in the vehicle." *Thornton*. In many cases, as when a recent occupant is arrested for a traffic violation, there will be no reasonable basis to believe the vehicle contains relevant evidence. See, e.g., *Atwater v. Lago Vista*, 532 U.S. 318 (2001); *Knowles v. Iowa*, 525 U.S. 113 (1998). But in others, including *Belton* and *Thornton*, the offense of arrest will supply a basis for searching the passenger compartment of an arrestee's vehicle and any containers therein. . . .

The State argues that *Belton* searches are reasonable regardless of the possibility of access in a given case because that expansive rule correctly balances law enforcement interests, including the interest in a bright-line rule, with an arrestee's limited privacy interest in his vehicle.

For several reasons, we reject the State's argument. First, the State seriously undervalues the privacy interests at stake. Although we have recognized that a motorist's privacy interest in his vehicle is less substantial than in his home, the former interest is nevertheless important and deserving of constitutional protection. It is particularly significant that *Belton* searches authorize police officers to search not just the passenger compartment but every purse, briefcase, or other container within that space. A rule that gives police the power to conduct such a search whenever an individual is caught committing a traffic offense, when there is no basis for believing evidence of the offense might be found in the vehicle, creates a serious and recurring threat to the privacy of countless individuals. Indeed, the character of that threat implicates the central concern underlying the Fourth Amendment—the concern about giving police officers unbridled discretion to rummage at will among a person's private effects.

At the same time as it undervalues these privacy concerns, the State exaggerates the clarity that its reading of *Belton* provides. Courts that have read *Belton* expansively are at odds regarding how close in time to the arrest and how proximate to the arrestee's vehicle an officer's first contact with the arrestee must be to bring the encounter within *Belton*'s purview and whether a search is reasonable when it commences or continues after the arrestee has been removed from the scene. The rule has thus generated a great deal of uncertainty, particularly for a rule touted as providing a "bright line."

Contrary to the State's suggestion, a broad reading of *Belton* is also unnecessary to protect law enforcement safety and evidentiary interests. Under our view, *Belton* and *Thornton* permit an officer to conduct a vehicle search when an arrestee is within reaching distance of the vehicle or it is reasonable to believe the vehicle contains evidence of the offense of arrest. Other established exceptions to the warrant requirement authorize a vehicle search under additional circumstances when safety or evidentiary concerns demand. For instance, *Michigan v. Long*, 463 U.S. 1032 (1983), permits an officer to search a vehicle's passenger compartment when he has reasonable suspicion that an individual, whether or not the arrestee, is "dangerous" and might access the vehicle to "gain immediate control of weapons." If there is probable cause to believe a vehicle contains evidence of criminal activity, *United States v. Ross*, 456 U.S. 798 (1982), authorizes a search of any area of the vehicle in which the evidence might be found. Unlike the searches permitted by Justice SCALIA's opinion concurring in the judgment in *Thornton*, which we conclude today are reasonable for purposes of the Fourth Amendment, *Ross* allows searches for evidence relevant to offenses other than the offense of arrest, and the scope of the search authorized is broader. Finally, there may be still other circumstances in which safety or evidentiary interests would justify a search. *Maryland v. Buie*, 494 U.S. 325 (1990) (holding that, incident to arrest, an officer may conduct a limited protective sweep of those areas of a house in which he reasonably suspects a dangerous person may be hiding).

These exceptions together ensure that officers may search a vehicle when genuine safety or evidentiary concerns encountered during the arrest of a vehicle's recent occupant justify a search. Construing *Belton* broadly to allow vehicle searches incident to any arrest would serve no purpose except to provide a police entitlement, and it is anathema to the Fourth Amendment to permit a warrantless search on that basis. For these reasons, we are unpersuaded by the State's arguments that a broad reading of *Belton* would meaningfully further law enforcement interests and justify a substantial intrusion on individuals' privacy. . . .

Police may search a vehicle incident to a recent occupant's arrest only if the arrestee is within reaching distance of the passenger compartment at the time of the search or it is reasonable to believe the vehicle contains evidence of the offense of arrest. When these justifications are absent, a search of an arrestee's vehicle will be unreasonable unless police obtain a warrant or show that another exception to the warrant requirement applies. The Arizona Supreme Court correctly held that this case involved an unreasonable search. Accordingly, the judgment of the State Supreme Court is affirmed.

☐ *Justice SCALILA concurring.*

To determine what is an "unreasonable" search within the meaning of the Fourth Amendment, we look first to the historical practices the Framers sought to preserve; if those provide inadequate guidance, we apply traditional standards of reasonableness. Since the historical scope of officers' authority to search vehicles incident to arrest is uncertain, see *Thornton v. United States*, 541 U.S. 615 (2004) (SCALIA, J., concurring in judgment), traditional standards of reasonableness govern. It is abundantly clear that those standards do not justify what I take to be the rule set forth in *New York v. Belton*, 453 U.S. 454 (1981), and *Thornton*: that arresting officers may always search an arrestee's vehicle in order to protect themselves from hidden weapons. When an arrest is made in connection with a roadside stop, police virtually always have a less intrusive and more effective means of ensuring their safety—and a means that is virtually always employed: ordering the arrestee away from the vehicle, patting him down in the open, handcuffing him, and placing him in the squad car. . . .

It must be borne in mind that we are speaking here only of a rule automatically permitting a search when the driver or an occupant is arrested. Where no arrest is made, we have held that officers may search the car if they reasonably believe "the suspect is dangerous and . . . may gain immediate control of weapons." *Michigan v. Long*, 463 U.S. 1032 (1983). In the no-arrest case, the possibility of access to weapons in the vehicle always exists, since the driver or passenger will be allowed to return to the vehicle when the interrogation is completed. The rule of *Michigan v. Long* is not at issue here.

Justice STEVENS acknowledges that an officer-safety rationale cannot justify all vehicle searches-incident-to-arrest, but asserts that that is not the rule *Belton* and *Thornton* adopted. (As described above, I read those cases differently). Justice STEVENS would therefore retain the application of *Chimel v. California*, 395 U.S. 752 (1969), in the car-search context but would apply in the future what he believes our cases held in the past: that officers making a roadside stop may search the vehicle so long as the "arrestee is within reaching distance of the passenger compartment at the time of the search." I believe that this standard fails to provide the needed guidance to arresting officers and also leaves much room for manipulation, inviting officers to leave the scene unsecured (at least where dangerous suspects are not involved) in order to conduct a vehicle search. In my view we should simply abandon the *Belton-Thornton* charade of officer safety and overrule those cases. I would hold that a vehicle search-incident-to-arrest is *ipso facto* "reasonable" only when the object of the search is evidence of the crime for which the arrest was made, or of another crime that the officer has probable cause to believe occurred. Because respondent was arrested for driving without a license (a crime for which no evidence could be expected to be found in the vehicle), I would hold in the present case that the search was unlawful. . . .

No other Justice, however, shares my view that application of *Chimel* in this context should be entirely abandoned. It seems to me unacceptable for the Court to come forth with a 4-to-1-to-4 opinion that leaves the governing rule uncertain. I am therefore confronted with the choice of either leaving the current understanding of *Belton* and *Thornton* in effect, or acceding to what seems to me the artificial narrowing of those cases adopted by Justice STEVENS. The latter, as I have said, does not provide the degree of certainty I think desirable in this field; but the former opens the field to what I think are plainly unconstitutional searches—which is the greater evil. I therefore join the opinion of the Court.

☐ *Justice ALITO, with whom THE CHIEF JUSTICE and Justice KENNEDY join, and with whom Justice BREYER joins except as to Part II-E, dissenting.*

Twenty-eight years ago, in *New York v. Belton*, 453 U.S. 454 (1981), this Court held that "when a policeman has made a lawful custodial arrest of the occupant of an automobile, he may, as a contemporaneous incident of that arrest, search the passenger compartment of that automobile." Five years ago, in *Thornton v. United States*, 541 U.S. 615 (2004)—a case involving a situation not materially distinguishable from the situation here—the Court not only reaffirmed but extended the holding of *Belton*, making it applicable to recent occupants. Today's decision effectively overrules those important decisions, even though respondent Gant has not asked us to do so.

To take the place of the overruled precedents, the Court adopts a new two-part rule under which a police officer who arrests a vehicle occupant or recent occupant may search the passenger compartment if (1) the arrestee is within reaching distance of the vehicle at the time of the search or (2) the officer has reason to believe that the vehicle contains evidence of the offense of arrest. The first part of this new rule may endanger arresting officers and is truly endorsed by only four Justices; Justice SCALIA joins solely for the purpose of avoiding a "4-to-1-to-4 opinion." The second part of the new rule is taken from Justice SCALIA's separate opinion in *Thornton* without any independent explanation of its origin or justification and is virtually certain to confuse law enforcement officers and judges for some time to come. The Court's decision will cause the suppression of evidence gathered in many searches carried out in good-faith reliance on well-settled case law, and although the Court purports to base its analysis on the landmark decision in *Chimel v. California*, 395 U.S. 752 (1969), the Court's reasoning undermines *Chimel*. I would follow *Belton*, and I therefore respectfully dissent. . . .

The precise holding in *Belton* could not be clearer. The Court stated unequivocally: "[W]e hold that when a policeman has made a lawful custodial arrest of the occupant of an automobile, he may, as a contemporaneous incident of that arrest, search the passenger compartment of that automobile."

Despite this explicit statement, the opinion of the Court in the present case curiously suggests that *Belton* may reasonably be read as adopting a holding that is narrower than the one explicitly set out in the *Belton* opinion, namely, that an officer arresting a vehicle occupant may search the passenger compartment "when the passenger compartment is within an arrestee's reaching distance." According to the Court, the broader reading of *Belton* that has gained wide acceptance "may be attributable to Justice BRENNAN's dissent."

Contrary to the Court's suggestion, however, Justice BRENNAN's *Belton* dissent did not mischaracterize the Court's holding in that case or cause that holding to be misinterpreted. As noted, the *Belton* Court explicitly stated precisely what it held. . . .

Respondent in this case has not asked us to overrule *Belton*, much less *Chimel*. Respondent's argument rests entirely on an interpretation of *Belton* that is plainly incorrect, an interpretation that disregards *Belton's* explicit delineation of its holding. I would therefore leave any reexamination of our prior precedents for another day, if such a reexamination is to be undertaken at all. In this case, I would simply apply *Belton* and reverse the judgment below.

Virginia v. Moore
128 S.Ct. 1598 (2008)

Rather than issuing a summons required by Virginia law, police arrested David Moore for the misdemeanor of driving with a suspended license. A search incident to the arrest found crack cocaine and Moore was charged and tried on drug charges. The trial court rejected a motion to suppress the evidence on Fourth Amendment grounds and Moore was convicted. The Virginia state supreme court reversed, reasoning that the search violated the Fourth Amendment because the arresting officers should have issued a citation under state law, and the Fourth Amendment does not permit a search incident to an arrest for a traffic citation. Moore appealed and the Supreme Court granted review.

The state supreme court's decision was reversed by a unanimous Court. Justice Scalia delivered the opinion of the Court. Justice Ginsburg filed a concurring opinion.

☐ *Justice SCALIA delivered the opinion of the Court.*

We consider whether a police officer violates the Fourth Amendment by making an arrest based on probable cause but prohibited by state law.

On February 20, 2003, two City of Portsmouth police officers stopped a car driven by David Lee Moore. They had heard over the police radio that a person known as "Chubs" was driving with a suspended license, and one of the officers knew Moore by that nickname. The officers determined that Moore's license was in fact suspended, and arrested him for the misdemeanor of driving on a suspended license, which is punishable under Virginia law by a year in jail and a $2,500 fine. The officers subsequently searched Moore and found that he was carrying 16 grams of crack cocaine and $516 in cash. Under state law, the officers should have issued Moore a summons instead of arresting him. Driving on a suspended license, like some other misdemeanors, is not an arrestable offense except as to those who "fail or refuse to discontinue" the violation, and those whom the officer reasonably believes to be likely to disregard a summons, or likely to harm themselves or others. . . .

Moore was charged with possessing cocaine with the intent to distribute it in violation of Virginia law. He filed a pretrial motion to suppress the evidence from the arrest search. Virginia law does not, as a general matter, require suppression of evidence obtained in violation of state law. Moore argued, however, that suppression was required by the Fourth Amendment. The trial court denied the motion, and after a bench trial found Moore guilty of the drug charge and sentenced him to a 5-year prison term, with one year and six months of the sentence suspended. The conviction was reversed by a panel of Virginia's intermediate court on Fourth Amendment grounds, [but] reversed again by the Virginia Supreme Court. The Court reasoned that since the arresting officers should have issued Moore a citation under state law, and the Fourth Amendment does not permit search incident to citation, the arrest search violated the Fourth Amendment.

The Fourth Amendment protects "against unreasonable searches and seizures" of (among other things) the person. In determining whether a search or seizure is unreasonable, we begin with history. We look to the statutes and common law of the founding era to determine the norms that the Fourth Amendment was meant to preserve. See *Wyoming v. Houghton*, 526 U.S. 295 (1999). We are aware of no historical indication that those who ratified the Fourth Amendment understood it as a redundant guarantee of whatever limits on search and seizure legislatures might have enacted. The immediate object of the Fourth Amendment was to prohibit the general warrants and writs of assistance that English judges had employed against the colonists. That suggests, if anything, that founding-era citizens were skeptical of using the rules for search and seizure set by government actors as the index of reasonableness. . . .

Of course such a claim would not have been available against state officers, since the Fourth Amendment was a restriction only upon federal power. But early Congresses tied the arrest authority of federal officers to state laws of arrest. Moreover, even though several state constitutions also prohibited unreasonable searches and seizures, citizens who claimed officers had violated state restrictions on arrest did not claim that the violations also ran afoul of the state constitutions. The apparent absence of such litigation is particularly striking in light of the fact that searches incident to warrantless arrests (which is to say arrests in which the officer was not insulated from private suit) were, as one commentator has put it, "taken for granted" at the founding, as were warrantless arrests themselves. . . .

When history has not provided a conclusive answer, we have analyzed a search or seizure in light of traditional standards of reasonableness "by assessing, on the one hand, the degree to which it intrudes upon an individual's privacy and, on the other, the degree to which it is needed for the promotion of legitimate governmental interests." *Houghton*. That methodology provides no support for Moore's Fourth Amendment claim. In a long line of cases, we have said that when an officer has probable cause to believe a person committed even a minor crime in his presence, the balancing of private and public interests is not in doubt. The arrest is constitutionally reasonable.

Our decisions counsel against changing this calculus when a State chooses to protect privacy beyond the level that the Fourth Amendment requires. We have treated additional protections exclusively as matters of state law. . . .

We are convinced that the approach of our prior cases is correct, because an arrest based on probable cause serves interests that have long been seen as sufficient to justify the seizure. Arrest ensures that a suspect appears to answer charges and does not continue a crime, and it safeguards evidence and enables officers to conduct an in-custody investigation. Moore argues that a State has no interest in arrest when it has a policy against arresting for certain crimes. That is not so, because arrest will still ensure a suspect's appearance at trial, prevent him from continuing his offense, and enable officers to investigate the incident more thoroughly. State arrest restrictions are more accurately characterized as showing that the State values its interests in forgoing arrests more highly than its interests in making them, or as showing that the State places a higher premium on privacy than the Fourth Amendment requires. A State is free to prefer one search-and-seizure policy among the range of constitutionally permissible options, but its choice of a more restrictive option does not render the less restrictive ones unreasonable, and hence unconstitutional.

If we concluded otherwise, we would often frustrate rather than further state policy. Virginia chooses to protect individual privacy and dignity more than the Fourth Amendment requires, but it also chooses not to attach to violations of its arrest rules the potent remedies that federal courts have applied to Fourth Amendment violations. Virginia does not, for example, ordinarily exclude from criminal trials evidence obtained in violation of its statutes. Moore would allow Virginia to accord enhanced protection against arrest only on pain of accompanying that protection with federal remedies for Fourth Amendment violations, which often include the exclusionary rule. States unwilling to lose control over the remedy would have to abandon restrictions on arrest altogether. This is an odd consequence of a provision designed to protect against searches and seizures.

Even if we thought that state law changed the nature of the Commonwealth's interests for purposes of the Fourth Amendment, we would adhere to the probable-cause standard. In determining what is reasonable under the Fourth Amendment, we have given great weight to the "essential interest in readily administrable rules." . . .

Finally, linking Fourth Amendment protections to state law would cause them to "vary from place to place and from time to time." Even at the same place and time, the Fourth Amendment's protections might vary if federal officers were not subject to the same statutory constraints as state officers. In *Elkins v. United States*, 364 U.S. 206 (1960), we noted the practical difficulties posed by the "silver-platter doctrine," which had imposed more stringent limitations on federal officers than on state police acting independent of them. It would be strange to construe a constitutional provision that did not apply to the States at all when it was adopted to now restrict state officers more than federal officers, solely because the States have passed search-and-seizure laws that are the prerogative of independent sovereigns.

We conclude that warrantless arrests for crimes committed in the presence of an arresting officer are reasonable under the Constitution, and that while States are free to regulate such arrests however they desire, state restrictions do not alter the Fourth Amendment's protections.

Moore argues that even if the Constitution allowed his arrest, it did not allow the arresting officers to search him. We have recognized, however, that officers may perform searches incident to constitutionally permissible arrests in order to ensure their safety and safeguard evidence. *United States v. Robinson*, 414 U.S. 218 (1973). We have described this rule as covering any "lawful arrest," with constitutional law as the reference point. . . .

The interests justifying search are present whenever an officer makes an arrest. A search enables officers to safeguard evidence, and, most critically, to ensure their safety during "the extended exposure which follows the taking of a suspect into custody and transporting him to the police station." *Robinson.*

Officers issuing citations do not face the same danger, and we therefore held in *Knowles v. Iowa*, 525 U.S. 113 (1998), that they do not have the same authority to search. We cannot agree with the Virginia Supreme Court that *Knowles* controls here. The state officers arrested Moore, and therefore faced the risks that are "an adequate basis for treating all custodial arrests alike for purposes of search justification." *Robinson.*

The Virginia Supreme Court may have concluded that *Knowles* required the exclusion of evidence seized from Moore because, under state law, the officers who arrested Moore should have issued him a citation instead. This argument might have force if the Constitution forbade Moore's arrest, because we have sometimes excluded evidence obtained through unconstitutional methods in order to deter constitutional violations. But the arrest rules that the officers violated were those of state law alone, and as we have just concluded, it is not the province of the Fourth Amendment to enforce state law. That Amendment does not require the exclusion of evidence obtained from a constitutionally permissible arrest. We reaffirm against a novel challenge what we have signaled for more than half a century. When officers have probable cause to believe that a person has committed a crime in their presence, the Fourth Amendment permits them to make an arrest, and to search the suspect in order to safeguard evidence and ensure their own safety. The judgment of the Supreme Court of Virginia is reversed, and the case is remanded for further proceedings not inconsistent with this opinion.

☐ *Justice GINSBURG, concurring in the judgment.*

I find in the historical record more support for Moore's position than the Court does. Further, our decision in *United States v. Di Re*, 332 U.S. 581 (1948), requiring suppression of evidence gained in a search incident to an unlawful arrest, seems to me pinned to the Fourth Amendment and not to our "supervisory power." And I am aware of no "long line of cases" holding that, regardless of state law, probable cause renders every warrantless arrest for crimes committed in the presence of an arresting officer "constitutionally reasonable."

I agree with the Court's conclusion and its reasoning, however, to this extent. In line with the Court's decision in *Atwater v. Lago Vista*, 532 U.S. 318 (2001), may bring a tort suit against the officer. But Virginia law does not demand the suppression of evidence seized. Virginia could have made driving on a suspended license an arrestable offense. The Commonwealth chose not to do so. Moore asks us to credit Virginia law on a police officer's arrest authority, but only in part. He emphasizes Virginia's classification of driving on a suspended license as a nonarrestable misdemeanor. Moore would have us ignore, however, the limited consequences Virginia attaches to a police officer's failure to follow the Commonwealth's summons-only instruction. For such an infraction, the officer may be disciplined and the person arrested by an officer who arrests when he should have issued a summons.

The Fourth Amendment, today's decision holds, does not put States to an all-or-nothing choice in this regard. A State may accord protection against arrest beyond what the Fourth Amendment requires, yet restrict the remedies available when police deny to persons they apprehend the extra protection state law orders. Because I agree that the arrest and search Moore challenges violated Virginia law, but did not violate the Fourth Amendment, I join the Court's judgment.

D | *Other Governmental Searches in the Administrative State*

Safford Unified School District No. 1 v. Redding
129 S.Ct. 2633 (2009)

The facts are discussed in the excerpt below. The Court affirmed the Court of Appeals for the Ninth Circuit's holding that a strip search of a middle school student for Ibuprofen pills violated the Fourth Amendment, but reversed the appellate court's holding that school officials did not enjoin qualified immunity from a suit for damages for violating constitutional rights.

Justice Souter delivered the opinion for the Court. Justices Stevens, Ginsburg, and Thomas each issued separate opinions, in part concurring and dissenting.

☐ *Justice SOUTER delivered the opinion of the Court.*

The issue here is whether a 13-year-old student's Fourth Amendment right was violated when she was subjected to a search of her bra and underpants by school officials acting on reasonable suspicion that she had brought forbidden prescription and over-the-counter drugs to school. Because there were no reasons to suspect the drugs presented a danger or were concealed in her underwear, we hold that the search did violate the Constitution, but because there is reason to question the clarity with which the right was established, the official who ordered the unconstitutional search is entitled to qualified immunity from liability.

The events immediately prior to the search in question began in 13-year-old Savana Redding's math class at Safford Middle School one October day in 2003. The assistant principal of the school, Kerry Wilson, came into the room and asked Savana to go to his office. There, he showed her a day planner, unzipped and open flat on his desk, in which there were several knives, lighters, a permanent marker, and a cigarette. Wilson asked Savana whether the planner was hers; she said it was, but that a few days before she had lent it to her friend, Marissa Glines. Savana stated that none of the items in the planner belonged to her.

Wilson then showed Savana four white prescription-strength ibuprofen 400-mg pills, and one over-the-counter blue naproxen 200-mg pill, all used for pain and inflammation but banned under school rules without advance permission. He asked Savana if she knew anything about the pills. Savana answered that she did not. Wilson then told Savana that he had received a report that she was giving these pills to fellow students; Savana denied it and agreed to let Wilson search her belongings. Helen Romero, an administrative assistant, came into the office, and together with Wilson they searched Savana's backpack, finding nothing.

At that point, Wilson instructed Romero to take Savana to the school nurse's office to search her clothes for pills. Romero and the nurse, Peggy Schwallier, asked Savana to remove her jacket, socks, and shoes, leaving her in stretch pants and a T-shirt (both without pockets), which she was then asked to remove. Finally, Savana was told to pull her bra out and to the side and shake it, and to pull out the elastic on her underpants, thus exposing her breasts and pelvic area to some degree. No pills were found.

Savana's mother filed suit against Safford Unified School District No. 1, Wilson, Romero, and Schwallier for conducting a strip search in violation of Savana's Fourth Amendment rights. The individuals (hereinafter petitioners) moved for summary judgment, raising a defense of qualified immunity. The District Court for the District of Arizona granted the motion on the ground that there was no Fourth Amendment violation, and a panel of the Ninth Circuit affirmed.

A closely divided Circuit sitting *en banc*, however, reversed. Following the two-step protocol for evaluating claims of qualified immunity, the Ninth Circuit held that the strip search was unjustified under the Fourth Amendment test for searches of children by school officials set out in *New Jersey v. T. L. O.*, 469 U.S. 325 (1985). . . .

In *T. L. O.*, we recognized that the school setting "requires some modification of the level of suspicion of illicit activity needed to justify a search," and held that for searches by school officials "a careful balancing of governmental and private interests suggests that the public interest is best served by a Fourth Amendment standard of reasonableness that stops short of probable cause." We have thus applied a standard of reasonable suspicion to determine the legality of a school administrator's search of a student, and have held that a school search "will be permissible in its scope when the measures adopted are reasonably related to the objectives of the search and not excessively intrusive in light of the age and sex of the student and the nature of the infraction." . . .

In this case, the school's policies strictly prohibit the nonmedical use, possession, or sale of any drug on school grounds, including "'[a]ny prescription or over-the-counter drug, except those for which permission to use in school has been granted pursuant to Board policy.'" A week before Savana was searched, another student, Jordan Romero (no relation of the school's administrative assistant), told the principal and Assistant Principal Wilson that "certain students were bringing drugs and weapons on campus," and that he had been sick after taking some pills that "he got from a classmate." On the morning of October 8, the same boy handed Wilson a white pill that he said Marissa Glines had given him. He told Wilson that students were planning to take the pills at lunch.

Wilson learned from Peggy Schwallier, the school nurse, that the pill was Ibuprofen 400 mg, available only by prescription. Wilson then called Marissa out of class. Outside the classroom, Marissa's teacher handed Wilson the day planner, found within Marissa's reach, containing various contraband items. Wilson escorted Marissa back to his office.

In the presence of Helen Romero, Wilson requested Marissa to turn out her pockets and open her wallet. Marissa produced a blue pill, several white ones, and a razor blade. Wilson asked where the blue pill came from, and Marissa answered, "'I guess it slipped in when she gave me the IBU 400s.'" When Wilson asked whom she meant, Marissa replied, "'Savana Redding.'" Wilson then enquired about the day planner and its contents; Marissa denied knowing anything about them. Wilson did not ask Marissa any followup questions to determine whether there was any likelihood that Savana presently had pills: neither asking when Marissa received the pills from Savana nor where Savana might be hiding them.

Schwallier did not immediately recognize the blue pill, but information provided through a poison control hotline indicated that the pill was a 200-mg dose of an antiinflammatory drug, generically called naproxen, available over the counter. At Wilson's direction, Marissa was then subjected to a search of her bra and underpants by Romero and Schwallier, as Savana was later on. The search revealed no additional pills.

It was at this juncture that Wilson called Savana into his office and showed her the day planner. Their conversation established that Savana and Marissa were on friendly terms: while she denied knowledge of the contraband, Savana admitted that the day planner was hers and that she had lent it to Marissa. Wilson had other reports of their friendship from staff members, who had identified Savana and Marissa as part of an unusually rowdy group at the school's opening dance in August, during which alcohol and cigarettes were found in the girls' bathroom. Wilson had reason to connect the girls with this contraband, for Wilson knew that Jordan Romero had told the principal that before the dance, he had been at a party at Savana's house where alcohol was served. Marissa's statement that the pills came from Savana was thus sufficiently plausible to warrant suspicion that Savana was involved in pill distribution.

This suspicion of Wilson's was enough to justify a search of Savana's backpack and outer clothing. If a student is reasonably suspected of giving out contraband pills, she is reasonably suspected of carrying them on her person and in the carryall that has become an item of student uniform in most places today. If Wilson's reasonable suspicion of pill distribution were not understood to support searches of outer clothes and backpack, it would not justify any search worth making. And the look into Savana's bag, in her presence and in the relative privacy of Wilson's office, was not excessively intrusive, any more than Romero's subsequent search of her outer clothing.

Here it is that the parties part company, with Savana's claim that extending the search at Wilson's behest to the point of making her pull out her underwear was constitutionally unreasonable. The exact label for this final step in the intrusion is not important, though strip search is a fair way to speak of it. Romero and Schwallier directed Savana to remove her clothes down to her underwear, and then "pull out" her bra and the elastic band on her underpants. Although Romero and Schwallier stated that they did not see anything when Savana followed their instructions, we would not define strip search and its Fourth Amendment consequences in a way that would guarantee litigation about who was looking and how much was seen. The very fact of Savana's pulling her underwear away from her body in the presence of the two officials who were able to see her necessarily exposed her breasts and pelvic area to some degree, and both subjective and reasonable societal expectations of personal privacy support the treatment of such a search as categorically distinct, requiring distinct elements of justification on the part of school authorities for going beyond a search of outer clothing and belongings.

Savana's subjective expectation of privacy against such a search is inherent in her account of it as embarrassing, frightening, and humiliating. The reasonableness of her expectation (required by the Fourth Amendment standard) is indicated by the consistent experiences of other young people similarly searched, whose adolescent vulnerability intensifies the patent intrusiveness of the exposure.

The indignity of the search does not, of course, outlaw it, but it does implicate the rule of reasonableness as stated in *T. L. O.*, that "the search as actually conducted [be] reasonably related in scope to the circumstances which justified the interference in the first place." The scope will be permissible, that is, when it is "not excessively intrusive in light of the age and sex of the student and the nature of the infraction."

Here, the content of the suspicion failed to match the degree of intrusion. Wilson knew beforehand that the pills were prescription-strength ibuprofen and over-the-counter naproxen, common pain relievers equivalent to two Advil, or one Aleve. He must have been aware of the nature and limited threat of the specific drugs he was searching for, and while just about anything can be taken in quantities that will do real harm, Wilson had no reason to suspect that large amounts of the drugs were being passed around, or that individual students were receiving great numbers of pills.

Nor could Wilson have suspected that Savana was hiding common painkillers in her underwear. . . .

In sum, what was missing from the suspected facts that pointed to Savana was any indication of danger to the students from the power of the drugs or their quantity, and any reason to suppose that Savana was carrying pills in her underwear. We think that the combination of these deficiencies was fatal to finding the search reasonable.

We do mean . . . to make it clear that the concern to limit a school search to reasonable scope requires the support of reasonable suspicion of danger or of resort to underwear for hiding evidence of wrongdoing before a search can reasonably make the quantum leap from outer clothes and backpacks to exposure of intimate parts. The meaning of such a search, and the degradation its subject may reasonably feel, place a search that intrusive in a category of its own demanding its own specific suspicions. . . .

☐ *Justice STEVENS, with whom Justice GINSBURG joins, concurring in part and dissenting in part.*

In *New Jersey v. T. L. O.*, 469 U.S. 325 (1985), the Court established a two-step inquiry for determining the reasonableness of a school official's decision to search a student. First, the Court explained, the search must be "'justified at its inception'" by the presence of "reasonable grounds for suspecting that the search will turn up evidence that the student has violated or is violating either the law or the rules of the school." Second, the search must be "permissible in its scope," which is achieved "when the measures adopted are reasonably related to the objectives of the search and not excessively intrusive in light of the age and sex of the student and the nature of the infraction."

Nothing the Court decides today alters this basic framework. It simply applies *T. L. O.* to declare unconstitutional a strip search of a 13-year-old honors student that was based on a groundless suspicion that she might be hiding medicine in her underwear. This is, in essence, a case in which clearly established law meets clearly outrageous conduct. I have long believed that "'[i]t does not require a constitutional scholar to conclude that a nude search of a 13-year-old child is an invasion of constitutional rights of some magnitude.'" The strip search of Savana Redding in this case was both more intrusive and less justified than the search of the student's purse in *T. L. O.* . . .

☐ *Justice THOMAS, concurring in the judgment in part and dissenting in part.*

I agree with the Court that the judgment against the school officials with respect to qualified immunity should be reversed. Unlike the majority, however, I would hold that the search of Savana Redding did not violate the Fourth Amendment. The majority imposes a vague and amorphous standard on school administrators. It also grants judges sweeping authority to second-guess the measures that these officials take to maintain discipline in their schools and ensure the health and safety of the students in their charge. This deep intrusion into the administration of public schools exemplifies why the Court should return to the common-law doctrine of *in loco parentis* under which "the judiciary was reluctant to interfere in the routine business of school administration, allowing schools and teachers to set and enforce rules and to maintain order." *Morse v. Frederick*, 551 U.S. 393 (2007) (THOMAS, J., concurring). But even under the prevailing Fourth Amendment test established by *New Jersey v. T. L. O.* (1985), all petitioners, including the school district, are entitled to judgment as a matter of law in their favor.

"Although the underlying command of the Fourth Amendment is always that searches and seizures be reasonable, what is reasonable depends on the context within which a search takes place." Thus, although public school students retain Fourth Amendment rights under this Court's precedent, those rights "are different . . . than elsewhere; the 'reasonableness' inquiry cannot disregard the schools' custodial and tutelary responsibility for children," *Vernonia School Dist. 47J v. Acton*, 515 U.S. 646 (1995). For nearly 25 years this Court has understood that "[m]aintaining order in the classroom has never been easy, but in more recent years, school disorder has often taken particularly ugly forms: drug use and violent crime in the schools have become major social problems." In schools, "[e]vents calling for discipline are frequent occurrences and sometimes require immediate, effective action." *Goss v. Lopez*, 419 U.S. 565 (1975).

For this reason, school officials retain broad authority to protect students and preserve "order and a proper educational environment" under the Fourth Amendment. This authority requires that school officials be able to engage in the "close supervision of schoolchildren, as well as . . . enforc[e] rules against conduct that would be perfectly permissible if undertaken by an adult." Seeking to reconcile the Fourth Amendment with this unique public school setting, the Court in *T. L. O.* held that a school search is "reasonable" if it is "'justified at its inception'" and "'reasonably related in scope to the circumstances which justified the interference in the first place.'" . . .

F | *The Exclusionary Rule*

In an important ruling, a bare majority of the Court in *Herring v. United States* (2009) (excerpted below) held that negligent errors and illegal seizures do not automatically trigger the exclusionary rule. Writing for the Court, Chief Justice Roberts emphasized that "Our cases establish that suppression [of illegally obtained evidence] is not an automatic consequence of a Fourth Amendment violation. Instead, the question turns on the culpability of the police and the potential of exclusion to deter wrongful police conduct." In other words if police make an objectively reasonable mistake—i.e., are merely negligent—the exclusionary rule does not apply to whatever evidence is found. In so holding, the majority extended the "good faith" exception to ordinary police conduct; see *United States v. Leon* and *Massachusetts v. Sheppard* (1984) (excerpted in Vol. 2, Ch. 7) and *Arizona v. Evans* (1995) (excerpted in Vol. 2, Ch. 7). As Chief Justice Roberts put it: "To trigger the exclusionary rule, police conduct must be sufficiently deliberate that exclusion can meaningfully deter it, and sufficiently culpable that such deterrence is worth the price paid by the justice system. As laid out in our cases, the exclusionary rule serves to deter deliberate, reckless, or grossly negligent conduct, or in some circumstances recurring or systemic negligence."

Notably, Justice Kennedy cast the deciding vote in *Herring*, joining Justices Scalia, Thomas, Alito, and Chief Justice Roberts, in holding that the exclusionary rule does not apply to evidence obtained after an arrest even if the police had no basis for it in the first place. However, in *Corley v. United States* (2009) (excerpted in Vol. 2, Ch. 8), Justice Kennedy joined Justices Stevens, Souter, Ginsburg, and Breyer, in holding that, when federal agents do not bring a suspect before a judge for "presentment" within six hours of an arrest, a defendant's confession made six hours after an arrest should be excluded as evidence at trial.

In addition, in *Pearson v. Callahan*, 129 S.Ct. 808 (2009), the Roberts Court unanimously held that police may not be sued for entering a house without a warrant after receiving a signal from an informant on the inside that a drug transaction is taking place. Writing for the Court, Justice Alito observed that the law in this area was not "clearly established" and therefore police are immune from liability for entering the house without a warrant. Together, *Herring* and *Pearson* further cut back on the scope and application of the exclusionary rule.

Herring v. United States
129 S.Ct. 695 (2009)

In July 2004, police investigator Mark Anderson learned that Bennie Dean Herring had gone to the Coffee County Sheriff's Department to retrieve something from his impounded truck. Herring was no stranger to law enforcement, and Anderson asked the county's warrant clerk to check for any outstanding warrants for Herring's arrest. When she found none, Anderson asked the clerk to check with her counterpart in neighboring Dale County. After checking Dale County's computer database, the clerk replied that there was an active arrest warrant for Herring's failure to appear on a felony charge, and information was relayed to Anderson, while a request was made for a fax copy of the warrant as confirmation. Subsequently, Anderson and a deputy followed Herring as he left the impound lot, pulled him over, and arrested him. A search incident to the arrest revealed methamphetamine in his pocket and a pistol (which as a felon he could not possess) in his vehicle. There was, however, a mistake about the warrant. The Dale County sheriff's computer records are supposed to correspond to actual arrest warrants, which the office also maintains. But the clerk discovered that the warrant had been recalled five months earlier. Normally when a warrant is recalled the court clerk's office or a judge's chambers calls the clerk, who enters the information in the sheriff's computer database and disposes of the physical copy. For whatever reason, the information about the recall of the warrant for Herring did not appear in the database.

After Herring was indicted in federal district court for illegally possessing the gun and drugs, he moved to suppress the evidence on the ground that his initial arrest had been illegal because the warrant had been rescinded. A magistrate judge recommended denying the motion because the arresting officers had acted in a good-faith belief that the warrant was still outstanding. Thus, even if there were a Fourth Amendment violation, there was "no reason to believe that application of the exclusionary rule here would deter the occurrence of any future mistakes." The district court adopted that recommendation and the Court of Appeals for the Eleventh Circuit affirmed. Herring appealed that decision and the Supreme Court granted review.

The appellate court's decision was affirmed by a five-to-four vote. Chief Justice Roberts delivered the opinion for the Court. Justices Ginsburg and Breyer issued dissenting opinions, which Justices Stevens and Souter joined.

☐ *CHIEF JUSTICE ROBERTS delivered the opinion of the Court.*

The Fourth Amendment forbids "unreasonable searches and seizures," and this usually requires the police to have probable cause or a warrant before making an arrest. What if an officer reasonably believes there is an outstanding arrest warrant, but that belief turns out to be wrong because of a negligent bookkeeping error by another police employee? The parties here agree that the ensuing arrest is still a violation of the Fourth Amendment, but dispute whether contraband found during a search incident to that arrest must be excluded in a later prosecution.

Our cases establish that of isolated negligence attenuated from the arrest. We hold that in these circumstances the jury should not be barred from considering all the evidence. . . .

When a probable-cause determination was based on reasonable but mistaken assumptions, the person subjected to a search or seizure has not necessarily been the victim of a constitutional violation. The very phrase "probable cause" confirms that the Fourth Amendment does not demand all possible precision. And whether the error can be traced to a mistake by a state actor or some other source may bear on the analysis. For purposes of deciding this case, however, we accept the parties' assumption that there was a Fourth Amendment violation. The issue is whether the exclusionary rule should be applied.

The Fourth Amendment protects "[t]he right of the people to be secure in their persons, houses, papers, and effects, against unreasonable searches and seizures," but "contains no provision expressly precluding the use of evidence obtained in violation of its commands," *Arizona v. Evans*, 514 U.S. 1 (1995). Nonetheless, our decisions establish an exclusionary rule that, when applicable, forbids the use of improperly obtained evidence at trial. See, e.g., *Weeks v. United States*, 232 U.S. 383 (1914). We have stated that this judicially created rule is "designed to safeguard Fourth Amendment rights generally through its deterrent effect." *United States v. Calandra*, 414 U.S. 338 (1974).

In analyzing the applicability of the rule, [*United States v.*] *Leon* [468 U.S. 897 (1984)], admonished that we must consider the actions of all the police officers involved. The Coffee County officers did nothing improper. Indeed, the error was noticed so quickly because Coffee County requested a faxed confirmation of the warrant.

The Eleventh Circuit concluded, however, that somebody in Dale County should have updated the computer database to reflect the recall of the arrest warrant. The court also concluded that this error was negligent, but did not find it to be reckless or deliberate. That fact is crucial to our holding that this error is not enough by itself to require "the extreme sanction of exclusion."

The fact that a Fourth Amendment violation occurred—i.e., that a search or arrest was unreasonable—does not necessarily mean that the exclusionary rule applies. *Illinois v. Gates*, 462 U.S. 213 (1983). Indeed, exclusion "has always been our last resort, not our first impulse," *Hudson v. Michigan*, 547 U.S. 586 (2006), and our precedents establish important principles that constrain application of the exclusionary rule.

First, the exclusionary rule is not an individual right and applies only where it "'result[s] in appreciable deterrence.'" *Leon*. We have repeatedly rejected the argument that exclusion is a necessary consequence of a Fourth Amendment violation. *Leon, Evans*. Instead we have focused on the efficacy of the rule in deterring Fourth Amendment violations in the future. See *Calandra; Stone v. Powell*, 428 U.S. 465 (1976).

In addition, the benefits of deterrence must outweigh the costs. "[T]o the extent that application of the exclusionary rule could provide some incremental deterrent, that possible benefit must be weighed against [its] substantial social costs." *Illinois v. Krull*, 480 U.S. 340 (1987). The principal cost of applying the rule is, of course, letting guilty and possibly dangerous defendants go free—something that "offends basic concepts of the criminal justice system." *Leon*.

These principles are reflected in the holding of *Leon*: When police act under a warrant that is invalid for lack of probable cause, the exclusionary rule does not apply if the police acted "in objectively reasonable reliance" on the subsequently invalidated search warrant. We (perhaps confusingly) called this objectively reasonable reliance "good faith." In a companion case, *Massachusetts v. Sheppard*, 468 U.S. 981 (1984), we held that the exclusionary rule did not apply when a warrant was invalid because a judge forgot to make "clerical corrections" to it.

Shortly thereafter we extended these holdings to warrantless administrative searches performed in good-faith reliance on a statute later declared unconstitutional. Finally, in *Evans*, we applied this good-faith rule to police who reasonably relied on mistaken information in a court's database that an arrest warrant was outstanding. We held that a mistake made by a judicial employee could not give rise to exclusion for three reasons: The exclusionary rule was crafted to curb police rather than judicial misconduct; court employees were unlikely to try to subvert the Fourth Amendment; and "most important, there [was] no basis for believing that application of the exclusionary rule in [those] circumstances" would have any significant effect in deterring the errors. *Evans* left unresolved "whether the evidence should be suppressed if police personnel were responsible for the error," an issue not argued by the State in that case, but one that we now confront.

The extent to which the exclusionary rule is justified by these deterrence principles varies with the culpability of the law enforcement conduct. As we said in *Leon*, "an assessment of the flagrancy of the police misconduct constitutes an important step in the calculus" of applying the exclusionary rule. . . .

Indeed, the abuses that gave rise to the exclusionary rule featured intentional conduct that was patently unconstitutional. In *Weeks*, a foundational exclusionary rule case, the officers had broken into the defendant's home (using a key shown to them by a neighbor), confiscated incriminating papers, then returned again with a U.S. Marshal to confiscate even more. Not only did they have no search warrant, which the Court held was required, but they could not have gotten one had they tried. They were so lacking in sworn and particularized information that "not even an order of court would have justified such procedure."

Equally flagrant conduct was at issue in *Mapp v. Ohio*, 367 U.S. 643 (1961), which overruled *Wolf v. Colorado*, 338 U.S. 25 (1949), and extended the exclusionary rule to the States. Officers forced open a door to Ms. Mapp's house, kept her lawyer from entering, brandished what the court concluded was a false warrant, then forced her into handcuffs and canvassed the house for obscenity. An error that arises from nonrecurring and attenuated negligence is thus far removed from the core concerns that led us to adopt the rule in the first place. And in fact since *Leon*, we have never applied the rule to exclude evidence obtained in violation of the Fourth Amendment, where the police conduct was no more intentional or culpable than this.

To trigger the exclusionary rule, police conduct must be sufficiently deliberate that exclusion can meaningfully deter it, and sufficiently culpable that such deterrence is worth the price paid by the justice system. As laid out in our cases, the exclusionary rule serves to deter deliberate, reckless, or grossly negligent conduct, or in some circumstances recurring or systemic negligence. The error in this case does not rise to that level.

Our decision in *Franks v. Delaware*, 438 U.S. 154 (1978), provides an analogy. In *Franks*, we held that police negligence in obtaining a warrant did not even rise to the level of a Fourth Amendment violation, let alone meet the more stringent test for triggering the exclusionary rule. We held that the Constitution allowed defendants, in some circumstances, "to challenge the truthfulness of factual statements made in an affidavit supporting the warrant," even after the warrant had issued. If those false statements were necessary to the Magistrate Judge's probable-cause determination, the warrant would be "voided." But we did not find all false statements relevant: "There must be allegations of deliberate falsehood or of reckless disregard for the truth," and "[a]llegations of negligence or innocent mistake are insufficient."

Both this case and *Franks* concern false information provided by police. Under *Franks*, negligent police miscommunications in the course of acquiring a warrant do not provide a basis to rescind a warrant and render a search or arrest invalid. Here, the miscommunications occurred in a different context—after the warrant had been issued and recalled—but that fact should not require excluding the evidence obtained.

The pertinent analysis of deterrence and culpability is objective, not an "inquiry into the subjective awareness of arresting officers." We have already held that "our good-faith inquiry is confined to the objectively ascertainable question whether a reasonably well trained officer would have known that the search was illegal" in light of "all of the circumstances." *Leon*. These circumstances frequently include a particular officer's knowledge and experience, but that does not make the test any more subjective than the one for probable cause, which looks to an officer's knowledge and experience, but not his subjective intent.

We do not suggest that all recordkeeping errors by the police are immune from the exclusionary rule. In this case, however, the conduct at issue was not so objectively culpable as to require exclusion. In *Leon* we held that "the marginal or nonexistent benefits produced by suppressing evidence obtained in objectively reasonable reliance on a subsequently invalidated search warrant cannot justify the substantial costs of exclusion." The same is true when evidence is obtained in objectively reasonable reliance on a subsequently recalled warrant.

If the police have been shown to be reckless in maintaining a warrant system, or to have knowingly made false entries to lay the groundwork for future false arrests, exclusion would certainly be justified under our cases should such misconduct cause a Fourth Amendment violation. We said as much in *Leon*, explaining that an officer could not "obtain a warrant on the basis of a 'bare bones' affidavit and then rely on colleagues who are ignorant of the circumstances under which the warrant was obtained to conduct the search."

The dissent also adverts to the possible unreliability of a number of databases not relevant to this case. In a case where systemic errors were demonstrated, it might be reckless for officers to rely on an unreliable warrant system. But there is no evidence that errors in Dale County's system are routine or widespread. . . .

Petitioner's claim that police negligence automatically triggers suppression cannot be squared with the principles underlying the exclusionary rule, as they have been explained in our cases. In light of our repeated holdings that the deterrent effect of suppression must be substantial and outweigh any harm to the justice system, we conclude that when police mistakes are the result of negligence such as that described here, rather than systemic error or reckless disregard of constitutional requirements, any marginal deterrence does not "pay its way." In such a case, the criminal should not "go free because the constable has blundered." *People v. Defore*, 242 N.Y. 13 (1926) (opinion of the Court by CARDOZO, J.).

☐ *Justice GINSBURG, with whom Justice STEVENS, Justice SOUTER, and Justice BREYER join, dissenting.*

The exclusionary rule provides redress for Fourth Amendment violations by placing the government in the position it would have been in had there been no unconstitutional arrest and search. The rule thus strongly encourages police compliance with the Fourth Amendment in the future. The Court, however, holds the rule inapplicable because careless recordkeeping by the police—not flagrant or deliberate misconduct—accounts for Herring's arrest.

I would not so constrict the domain of the exclusionary rule and would hold the rule dispositive of this case: "[I]f courts are to have any power to discourage [police] error of [the kind here at issue], it must be through the application of the exclusionary rule." *Arizona v. Evans*, 514 U.S. 1 (1995) (STEVENS, J., dissenting). The unlawful search in this case was contested in court because the police found methamphetamine in Herring's pocket and a pistol in his truck. But the "most serious impact" of the Court's holding will be on innocent persons "wrongfully arrested based on erroneous information [carelessly maintained] in a computer data base." . . .

Beyond doubt, a main objective of the rule "is to deter—to compel respect for the constitutional guaranty in the only effectively available way— by removing the incentive to disregard it." *Elkins v. United States*, 364 U.S. 206 (1960). But the rule also serves other important purposes: It "enabl[es] the judiciary to avoid the taint of partnership in official lawlessness," and it "assur[es] the people—all potential victims of unlawful government conduct—that the government would not profit from its lawless behavior, thus minimizing the risk of seriously undermining popular trust in government." *United States v. Calandra*, 414 U.S. 338 (1974) (BRENNAN, J., dissenting).

The Court maintains that Herring's case is one in which the exclusionary rule could have scant deterrent effect and therefore would not "pay its way." I disagree.

The exclusionary rule, the Court suggests, is capable of only marginal deterrence when the misconduct at issue is merely careless, not intentional or reckless. The suggestion runs counter to a foundational premise of tort law—that liability for negligence, i.e., lack of due care, creates an incentive to act with greater care. The Government so acknowledges.

That the mistake here involved the failure to make a computer entry hardly means that application of the exclusionary rule would have minimal value.

Consider the potential impact of a decision applying the exclusionary rule in this case. As earlier observed, the record indicates that there is no electronic connection between the warrant database of the Dale County Sheriff's Department and that of the County Circuit Clerk's office, which is located in the basement of the same building. When a warrant is recalled, one of the "many different people that have access to th[e] warrants," must find the hard copy of the warrant in the "two or three different places" where the department houses warrants, return it to the Clerk's office, and manually update the Department's database. The record reflects no routine practice of checking the database for accuracy, and the failure to remove the entry for Herring's warrant was not discovered until Investigator Anderson sought to pursue Herring five months later. Is it not altogether obvious that the Department could take further precautions to ensure the integrity of its database? The Sheriff's Department "is in a position to remedy the situation and might well do so if the exclusionary rule is there to remove the incentive to do otherwise."

Is the potential deterrence here worth the costs it imposes? In light of the paramount importance of accurate recordkeeping in law enforcement, I would answer yes, and next explain why, as I see it, Herring's motion presents a particularly strong case for suppression.

Electronic databases form the nervous system of contemporary criminal justice operations. In recent years, their breadth and influence have dramatically expanded. Police today can access databases that include not only the updated National Crime Information Center (NCIC), but also terrorist watch-lists, the Federal Government's employee eligibility system, and various commercial databases. . . . As a result, law enforcement has an increasing supply of information within its easy electronic reach.

The risk of error stemming from these databases is not slim. Herring's *amici* warn that law enforcement databases are insufficiently monitored and often out of date. Government reports describe, for example, flaws in NCIC databases, terrorist watchlist databases, and databases associated with the Federal Government's employment eligibility verification system.

Inaccuracies in expansive, interconnected collections of electronic information raise grave concerns for individual liberty. . . .

First, by restricting suppression to bookkeeping errors that are deliberate or reckless, the majority leaves Herring, and others like him, with no remedy for violations of their constitutional rights. There can be no serious assertion that relief is available under 42 U.S.C. Section 1983. The arresting officer would be sheltered by qualified immunity, and the police department itself is not liable for the negligent acts of its employees. Moreover, identifying the department employee who committed the error may be impossible.

Second, I doubt that police forces already possess sufficient incentives to maintain up-to-date records. The Government argues that police have no desire to send officers out on arrests unnecessarily, because arrests consume resources and place officers in danger. The facts of this case do not fit that description of police motivation. Here the officer wanted to arrest Herring and consulted the Department's records to legitimate his predisposition.

Third, even when deliberate or reckless conduct is afoot, the Court's assurance will often be an empty promise: How is an impecunious defendant to make the required showing? If the answer is that a defendant is entitled to discovery (and if necessary, an audit of police databases), then the Court has imposed a considerable administrative burden on courts and law enforcement.

Negligent recordkeeping errors by law enforcement threaten individual liberty, are susceptible to deterrence by the exclusionary rule, and cannot be remedied effectively through other means. Such errors present no occasion to further erode the exclusionary rule. The rule "is needed to make the Fourth Amendment something real; a guarantee that does not carry with it the exclusion of evidence obtained by its violation is a chimera." *Calandra.* (BRENNAN, J., dissenting). In keeping with the rule's "core concerns" suppression should have attended the unconstitutional search in this case.

For the reasons stated, I would reverse the judgment of the Eleventh Circuit.

☐ *Justice BREYER, with whom Justice Souter joins, dissenting.*

I agree with Justice GINSBURG and join her dissent. I write separately to note one additional supporting factor that I believe important. In *Arizona v. Evans,* 514 U.S. 1 (1995), we held that recordkeeping errors made by a court clerk do not trigger the exclusionary rule, so long as the police reasonably relied upon the court clerk's recordkeeping. The rationale for our decision was premised on a distinction between judicial errors and police errors, and we gave several reasons for recognizing that distinction.

First, we noted that "the exclusionary rule was historically designed as a means of deterring police misconduct, not mistakes by court employees." Second, we found "no evidence that court employees are inclined to ignore or subvert the Fourth Amendment or that lawlessness among these actors requires application of the extreme sanction of exclusion." Third, we recognized that there was "no basis for believing that application of the exclusionary rule . . . [would] have a significant effect on court employees responsible for informing the police that a warrant has been quashed. Because court clerks are not adjuncts to the law enforcement team engaged in the often competitive enterprise of ferreting out crime, they have no stake in the outcome of particular criminal prosecutions." Taken together, these reasons explain why police recordkeeping errors should be treated differently than judicial ones. . . .

Distinguishing between police recordkeeping errors and judicial ones not only is consistent with our precedent, but also is far easier for courts to administer than THE CHIEF JUSTICE's case-by-case, multifactored inquiry into the degree of police culpability. I therefore would apply the exclusionary rule when police personnel are responsible for a recordkeeping error that results in a Fourth Amendment violation.

The need for a clear line, and the recognition of such a line in our precedent, are further reasons in support of the outcome that Justice GINSBURG's dissent would reach.

8

THE FIFTH AMENDMENT GUARANTEE AGAINST SELF-ACCUSATION

A | Coerced Confessions and Police Interrogations

A bare majority in *Corley v. United States*, 129 S.Ct. 1558 (2009), reaffirmed a "Warren Court" ruling that if federal agents wait too long to take a suspect to be informed of the charges against him, a confession is barred even if voluntary. In a controversial ruling in *Mallory v. United States*, 354 U.S. 449 (1957), Justice Frankfurter held for a unanimous Court that a confession given seven hours after an arrest could not be used if there was an "unnecessary delay" in presenting the suspect to a magistrate to learn of the charge. The decision reaffirmed *McNabb v. United States*, 318 U.S. 332 (1943), but along the ruling in *Miranda v. Arizona*, 384 U.S. 436 (1966) (excerpted in Vol. 2, Ch. 8), inspired a reaction and Congress enacted the Crime Control and Safe Streets Act of 1968, which sought to limit the *Mallory-McNabb* rule and *Miranda*. In *Dickerson v. United States*, 530 U.S. 428 (2000) (excerpted in Vol. 2, Ch. 8) the Rehnquist Court reaffirmed *Miranda* as a constitutional ruling. And in *Corley*, although not a constitutional ruling, reaffirmed *Mallory-McNabb* in holding that confessions made six hours after an arrest were impermissible and that Congress had not discarded *Mallory* but "merely [sought] to narrow" it. Thus, voluntary confessions to federal crimes may not be admitted into evidence if the suspect was not fairly soon after confessing taken to court.

In Justice Souter's words for the majority: "In a world without *McNabb-Mallory*, federal agents would be free to question suspects for extended periods before bringing them out in the open, and we have always known what custodial secrecy leads to . . . No one with any smattering of the history of the twentieth century dictatorships needs a lecture on the subject . . . and there is mounting empirical evidence that these pressures can induce a frightening high percentage of people to confess to crimes they never committed." Chief Justice Roberts and Justices Scalia, Thomas, and Alito dissented.

9

THE RIGHT TO COUNSEL AND OTHER PROCEDURAL GUARANTEES

A | *The Right to Counsel*

By a seven-to-two vote, the Court held in *Indiana v. Edwards*, 128 S.Ct. 2379 (2008), that states may require a criminal defendant who suffers from mental illness to have a court-appointed law at trial, rather than acting in his own defense, even when the defendant is deemed competent stand trial. Edwards, who suffered from schizophrenia, was deemed by the trial court competent to stand trial but not competent to defend himself. He appealed that ruling, arguing that it violated his Sixth Amendment right to counsel and the Court's holding in *Faretta v. California*, 422 U.S. 806 (1976), that a defendant deemed competent to stand trial has a right to self-representation. Justice Breyer delivered the opinion of the Court that declined to overrule *Faretta* on the ground that states have some flexibility and that there was "no empirical research" showing "that *Faretta*'s holding has proven counterproductive in practice" or that the right of representing one's self "furthers or inhibits" the fairness of a trial. Justices Scalia and Thomas dissented.

In another seven-to-two decision, the Roberts Court held that a defendant's incriminating statements made in violation of the Sixth Amendment right to counsel to a governmental informant in a prison cell may be used to impeach the defendant's trial testimony. Writing for the Court in *Kansas v. Ventris*, 129 S.Ct. 1841 (2009), Justice Scalia held that the core of the Sixth Amendment right to counsel is a trial right and covers pretrial interrogations only to ensure that the defendant has "effective representation by counsel at the only stage when legal aid and advice would help him." (quoting *Massiah v. United States*, 377 U.S. 201 [1964]). But, the right to be free of uncounseled interrogation applies only at the time of police interrogation and not when a confession is admitted as evidence against the defendant. Justices Stevens and Ginsburg dissented.

Writing for a bare majority in *Montejo v. Louisiana*, 129 S.Ct. 2079 (2009), Justice Scalia also overturned a long-standing decision in *Michigan v. Jackson*, 475 U.S. 625 (1986), that barred police from initiating questions unless a suspect's lawyer is present. *Michigan v. Jackson* held that police may not question a suspect who has a lawyer or who has asked for one unless an attorney is present, even if a suspect agreed to talk with officers in the absence of an attorney. Writing for the Court in *Montejo*, Justice Scalia dismissed the prior ruling as "poorly reasoned" because police could not even ask a suspect who had been appointed an attorney if he wanted to talk. In his words: "It would be completely unjustified to presume that a defendant's consent to police-initiated interrogation was involuntary or coerced simply because he had previously been appointed a lawyer." Moreover, he added that, "The considerable adverse effect of this rule upon society's ability to solve crimes and bring criminals to justice far outweighs its capacity to prevent a genuinely coerced agreement to speak without counsel present." Dissenting Justice Stevens, who had delivered the decision in *Michigan v. Jackson*, joined by Justices Souter, Ginsburg, and Breyer, countered that "The police interrogation in this case clearly violated petitioner's Sixth Amendment right to counsel," and would "only diminish the public's confidence in the reliability and fairness of our system of justice." Jesse Jay Montejo was found guilty of killing Lewis Ferrari. He had been appointed an attorney but never indicated that he wanted the assistance of counsel. After being given his *Miranda* rights to remain silent and to have counsel, in the absence of counsel, he showed police where to look for the murder weapon. While in the police car en route, he also wrote a letter to Ferrari's widow incriminating himself. That letter was later used against him at trial and he was convicted and sentenced to death.

In its 2009–2010 term, the Court will also consider the scope of "*Miranda* rights" in *Florida v. Powell* (Docket No. 08–1175) and whether those warnings to a suspect in police custody may exclude an explicit assurance that the individual may have a lawyer in the room while under interrogation. Powell was arrested for the possession of a firearm and was initially read his rights, and he also signed a waiver of those rights. The form, however, did not expressly state that he had the right to have an attorney present while police asked him questions. During the interrogation he admitted that the gun was his. A state trial court allowed the introduction of the confession, but on appeal Powell's conviction was reversed on the ground that the warning was insufficient because it only informed Powell that he had a right to counsel before questioning began. The Florida state supreme court affirmed that decision, holding that the warning given to Powell was inadequate because it did not expressly notify him of his right to counsel during questioning.

B | *Plea Bargaining and the Right to Effective Counsel*

In its 2009–2010 term, the justices will consider whether the failure of counsel to present evidence of a defendant's mental impairment constitutes ineffective counsel under the Sixth Amendment, in *Wood v. Allen* (No. 08–9156). A jury convicted Wood of capital murder and a judge sentenced him to death for the killing of his girlfriend. He appealed, claiming that he is mentally retarded and cannot be executed under the Court's precedents, as well as that his counsel was ineffective in failing to present evidence of his low mental abilities. A state appellate and supreme court affirmed and the U.S. Supreme Court denied an appeal. But after a post-conviction court found that he was not mentally retarded and had effective counsel, Wood filed a petition for a writ of *habeas corpus* and a federal district court vacated his death sentence on the basis of ineffective counsel. On the state's appeal, the Court of Appeals for the Eleventh Circuit held that Wood was not mentally retarded and that he had had effective counsel. Wood appealed that decision and the Court granted review.

■ THE DEVELOPMENT OF LAW

Rulings on Plea Bargaining and Effective Counsel

CASE	VOTE	RULING
Wright v. VanPatten, 128 S.Ct. 743 (2008)	9:0	In a *per curiam* opinion, the Robert's Court held that during a plea bargaining hearing there was

no violation of the Sixth Amendment right to counsel when the defendant's lawyer was present only on a speaker phone.

D | *The Right to an Impartial Jury Trial*

In *Kimbrough v. United States*, 128 S.Ct. 558 (2007), the Court reaffirmed an earlier ruling in *United States v. Booker*, 543 U.S. 2220 (2005), that the federal mandatory sentencing guidelines were only advisory for federal judges in sentencing. In *Booker* a bare majority ruled that the federal mandatory sentencing guidelines violate the Sixth Amendment because federal judges may impose enhanced sentences based on facts that a jury did not consider. The Court was badly fragmented in *Booker*, however, and two opinions for the Court were delivered for different bare majorities. On the one hand, Justice Stevens, joined by Justices Scalia, Souter, Thomas, and Ginsburg, ruled that federal judges are no longer bound by the guidelines and that they were only advisory. On the other hand, Justice Breyer, joined by Chief Justice Rehnquist and Justices O'Connor, Kennedy, and Ginsburg, held that the guidelines should still be consulted and that judges' sentences are subject to reversal if appellate courts find them unreasonable and defendants deserve longer or shorter sentences. The federal guidelines, in the words of Justice Breyer, who helped write them, serve to "avoid excessive sentencing disparities while maintaining flexibility sufficient to individualize sentences where necessary." Justice Ginsburg cast the crucial fifth vote for both opinions but issued no separate opinion. Justices Stevens, Scalia, Thomas, and Breyer, each filed dissenting opinions.

Over the last decade a controversy emerged over the differential sentencing under the guidelines for those convicted of crack cocaine (who are predominantly African American) and powder cocaine (who are predominantly white). Writing for the Court in *Kimbrough*, Justice Ginsburg reasserted that the federal guidelines were only advisory, over the dissents of Justices Thomas and Alito. Kimbrough had been convicted of selling fifty grams of crack cocaine and subject to a sentence under the guidelines of 228 to 270 months in prison. But the district court found that excessive and sentenced him to 180 months in prisons and five years of supervised release. An appellate court vacated that sentence because it was outside the guidelines, but the Supreme Court reversed, holding that the guidelines are only advisory and that appellate courts must review the imposition of sentences under an "abuse of discretion standard," not the prescriptions of the guidelines.

In a related case the Court reinforced that ruling. In *Gall v. United States*, 128 S.Ct. 586 (2007), Justice Stevens writing for the Court, with Justices Thomas and Alito again dissenting, held that appellate courts must review all sentences under the "deferential abuse of discretion standard" regardless of the range of variance between the sentence imposed and the guidelines' recommendations. Gall had been sentenced, based on the district court's evaluation of all facts, to thirty-six months of probation instead of the recommended thirty to thirty-seven months of prison.

In its 2008–2009 term, the Court limited the line of cases following *Apprendi v. New Jersey*, 536 U.S. 466 (2000) (see Vol. 2, Ch. 9), which limited judges' discretion in sentencing in holding that enhanced sentences may not be imposed unless based on facts found by a jury. In *Oregon v. Ice*, 129 S.Ct. 711 (2009), a bare majority held that the Sixth Amendment jury trial right limited judges' discretion to decide to require that sentences be served separately rather than simultaneously. Thomas Ice was tried for assaulting an eleven-year-old girl and charged with entering her home twice and sexually touching her four times; he was convicted on all six counts. Under Oregon law, sentences for multiple crimes are served concurrently, but the trial judge found that the two charges of burglary and four sex crimes were separate incidents. The judge sentenced Ice to a total of 340 months in prison, with three of the six sentences running consecutively. Writing for a bare majority Justice Ginsburg reasoned that both historic practice—that juries traditionally had no role in deciding for or against concurrent sentences—and "respect for state sovereignty" justified confining the ruling in *Apprendi* to "sentences for discrete crimes." By contrast, dissenting Justice Scalia, joined by Chief Justice Roberts and Justices Souter and Thomas, countered that the majority's decision was "a virtual copy of the dissents" in the *Apprendi* line of rulings and that the matter of enhanced sentencing—in this case, consecutive (instead of concurrent) sentencing on convictions—was a matter for juries, not judges, to decide.

E | *A Speedy and Public Trial*

In *Vermont v. Brillon*, 129 S.Ct. 1283 (2009) the Court held that trial delays caused by defense counsel, whether privately retained or appointed by a court, are attributable to the defendant unless the delays are the result of a "systematic breakdown in the public defender system." At issue was whether a three-year delay in bringing a defendant to trial violated the Sixth Amendment right to a speedy trial. Brillon was arrested and charged with felony domestic violence and as a habitual offender. During the three years prior to his trial, he was assigned six different public defenders. He was eventually found guilty and sentenced to twelve to twenty years in prison, and he appealed. Writing for the Court, Justice Ginsburg ruled that assigned counsel "act on behalf of their clients, and delays sought by counsel are ordinarily attributable to the defendants they represent." In this case, all but six months of the delays were attributable to the defense counsel, and thus to the defendant; the only time delay caused by defense counsel attributable to the state was the result of a "systematic breakdown in the public defender system." Justice Breyer, joined by Justice Stevens, dissented.

F | *The Right to Be Informed of Charges and to Confront Accusers*

In a five-to-four ruling in *Melendez-Diaz v. Massachusetts*, 129 S.Ct. 2527 (2009), the majority held that chemists and other scientists who prepare crime lab reports may be summoned as witnesses in criminal trials to defend their analyses in order not to violate defendants' Sixth Amendment right to confront witnesses against them. Writing for the Court, Justice Scalia observed that "There is little reason to believe that confrontation will be useless in testing analysts' honesty, proficiency, and methodology—the features that are commonly the focus in a cross-examination of experts." In doing so, he recited reports about how defective crime labs and their results are and dismissed claims that crime lab reports are a product of "neutral scientific testing." "Forensic evidence," Justice Scalia wrote, "is not uniquely immune from the risk of manipulation." Chief Justice Roberts and Justices Kennedy, Breyer, and Alito dissented.

IO

CRUEL AND UNUSUAL PUNISHMENT

A | Noncapital Punishment

In its 2009–2010 term, the Roberts Court will consider whether a sentence of lifetime imprisonment, without the possibility of parole, for a nonhomicide crime committed by a juvenile violates the Eighth Amendment in two cases, *Sullivan v. Florida* (No. 08–7621) and *Graham v. Florida* (No. 08–7412). Joe Sullivan was tried and convicted for the rape and assault of a seventy-three-year-old woman in 1989. He was thirteen years old at the time and had been involved in a burglary with two other boys earlier in the day. Under Florida law he was sentenced to life in prison. A state appellate court affirmed his conviction without an opinion, and the state supreme court declined review without an opinion. Terrance Graham was on probation when he was tried and found guilty of robbery. At the time of the crime, he was seventeen years old. A state appeals court found that, although the imposition of the death penalty on a minor violates the Eighth Amendment, under *Roper v. Simmons*, 543 U.S. 551 (2005) (excerpted in Vol. 2, Ch. 10), a lifetime sentence for a juvenile is distinguishable and does not per se violate the cruel and unusual punishment clause. The state court of appeals further reasoned that even if such a sentence runs afoul of international norms, the U.S. Supreme Court has held that the courts, not the international community, determine the scope of Eighth Amendment protections.

B | *Capital Punishment*

In a sharply fragmented ruling, the Court concluded that the most common method of execution by lethal injection does not violate the Eighth Amendment. The vote was seven to two in *Baze v. Rees* (excerpted below), but the opinion for the Court failed to commend a majority. Writing for a plurality, joined by only Justices Kennedy and Alito, Chief Justice Roberts adopted as a standard for assessing the validity of an execution method whether it poses a "substantial risk of serious harm," and rejected the death row inmate's claim that the standard should be "unnecessary risk." Chief Justice Roberts's opinion left open the possibility of further challenges to the use of lethal drugs under a specific procedure of other states; lethal injection is used in thirty-five other states and the federal government. Notably, he observed that states are free to choose a procedure for carrying out executions so long as they are shown to be "feasible, readily implemented, and in fact significantly reduce a substantial risk of severe pain." But Chief Justice Roberts also added that "if a state refuses to adopt such an alternative in the face of these documented advantages, without a legitimate penological justification for adhering to its current method of execution, then a state's refusal to change its method can be viewed as 'cruel and unusual punishment' under the Eighth Amendment." In a concurring opinion, Justice Stevens contended that the ruling, instead of ending the controversy over the use of a three-drug protocol injection, would only invite more litigation. He also noted that based on his experience the imposition of capital punishment constituted a pointless and needless extinction of life with only negligible social benefits. Still, he would abide by the Court's precedents upholding capital punishment. In separate concurring opinions, Justices Scalia, Thomas, and Alito took issue with both Chief Justice Roberts's and Justice Stevens's opinions. Justice Ginsburg, joined by Justice Souter, filed a dissenting opinion.

In an even more sharply divided ruling, a bare majority struck down death penalty laws in Louisiana and five other states that imposed capital punishment for crimes like child rape. Writing for the majority in *Kennedy v. Louisiana* (2008) (excerpted below), Justice Kennedy categorically ruled out the death penalty for individual crimes "where the victim's life was not taken" but did not rule out capital punishment for "offenses against the state" such as treason, terrorism, or espionage. The Court had previously overruled laws imposing the death penalty for the crime of rape of an adult woman as disproportionate to the offense, in *Coker v. Georgia*, 433 U.S. 548 (1977). Justice Kennedy based the decision on "evolving standards of decency" and the Court's "own independent judgment." Writing for the dissenters, Justice Alito, joined by Chief Justice Roberts and Justices Scalia and Thomas, sharply criticized the majority's reasoning and maintained that the issue should be left to the states.

Baze v. Rees
128 S.CT. 1530 (2008)

Ralph Baze and another death row inmate challenged the constitutionality of Kentucky's method of lethal injection by a three-drug protocol on the ground that it did not necessarily ensure a painless execution. A state court rejected the claim, and the Kentucky Supreme Court affirmed, though noting that a method of execution violates the Eighth Amendment if it "creates a substantial risk of wanton and unnecessary infliction of pain, torture, or lingering death." Baze appealed that decision and the Supreme Court granted *certiorari*.

The state supreme court's decision was affirmed by a seven-to-two vote. Chief Justice Roberts delivered the opinion for the Court, which only Justices Kennedy and Alito joined. Justices Stevens, Scalia, Thomas, and Alito filed separate concurring opinions. Justice Ginsburg, joined by Justice Souter, filed a dissenting opinion.

☐ *CHIEF JUSTICE ROBERTS announced the judgment of the Court and delivered the opinion, in which Justice KENNEDY and Justice ALITO join.*

Like 35 other States and the Federal Government, Kentucky has chosen to impose capital punishment for certain crimes. As is true with respect to each of these States and the Federal Government, Kentucky has altered its method of execution over time to more humane means of carrying out the sentence. That progress has led to the use of lethal injection by every jurisdiction that imposes the death penalty.

Petitioners in this case—each convicted of double homicide—acknowledge that the lethal injection procedure, if applied as intended, will result in a humane death. They nevertheless contend that the lethal injection protocol is unconstitutional under the Eighth Amendment's ban on "cruel and unusual punishments," because of the risk that the protocol's terms might not be properly followed, resulting in significant pain. They propose an alternative protocol, one that they concede has not been adopted by any State and has never been tried. . . .

By the middle of the 19th century, "hanging was the 'nearly universal form of execution' in the United States." *Campbell v. Wood*, 511 U.S. 1119 (1994). In 1888, following the recommendation of a commission empaneled by the Governor to find " 'the most humane and practical method known to modern science of carrying into effect the sentence of death,' " New York became the first State to authorize electrocution as a form of capital punishment. *Glass v. Louisiana*, 471 U.S. 1080 (1985). By 1915, 11 other States had followed suit, motivated by the "well-grounded belief that electrocution is less painful and more humane than hanging." *Malloy v. South Carolina*, 237 U.S. 180 (1915).

Electrocution remained the predominant mode of execution for nearly a century, although several methods, including hanging, firing squad, and lethal gas were in use at one time. Following the 9-year hiatus in executions that ended with our decision in *Gregg v. Georgia*, 428 U.S. 153 (1976), however, state legislatures began responding to public calls to reexamine electrocution as a means of assuring a humane death. A total of 36 States have now adopted lethal injection as the exclusive or primary means of implementing the death penalty, making it by far the most prevalent method of execution in the United States. It is also the method used by the Federal Government.

Of these 36 States, at least 30 (including Kentucky) use the same combination of three drugs in their lethal injection protocols. The first drug, sodium thiopental (also known as Pentathol), is a fast-acting barbiturate sedative that induces a deep, coma like unconsciousness when given in the amounts used for lethal injection. The second drug, pancuronium bromide (also known as Pavulon), is a paralytic agent that inhibits all muscular-skeletal movements and, by paralyzing the diaphragm, stops respiration. Potassium chloride, the third drug, interferes with the electrical signals that stimulate the contractions of the heart, inducing cardiac arrest. The proper administration of the first drug ensures that the prisoner does not experience any pain associated with the paralysis and cardiac arrest caused by the second and third drugs.

Kentucky replaced electrocution with lethal injection in 1998. The Kentucky statute does not specify the drugs or categories of drugs to be used during an execution, instead mandating that "every death sentence shall be executed by continuous intravenous injection of a substance or combination of substances sufficient to cause death." . . .

Kentucky's execution facilities consist of the execution chamber, a control room separated by a one-way window, and a witness room. The warden and deputy warden remain in the execution chamber with the prisoner, who is strapped to a gurney. The execution team administers the drugs remotely from the control room through five feet of IV tubing. If, as determined by the warden and deputy warden through visual inspection, the prisoner is not unconscious within 60 seconds following the delivery of the sodium thiopental to the primary IV site, a new 3-gram dose of thiopental is administered to the secondary site before injecting the pancuronium and potassium chloride. In addition to assuring that the first dose of thiopental is successfully administered, the warden and deputy warden also watch for any problems with the IV catheters and tubing.

A physician is present to assist in any effort to revive the prisoner in the event of a last-minute stay of execution. By statute, however, the physician is prohibited from participating in the "conduct of an execution," except to certify the cause of death. . . .

The Eighth Amendment to the Constitution, applicable to the States through the Due Process Clause of the Fourteenth Amendment, see *Robinson v. California*, 370 U.S. 660 (1962), provides that "[e]xcessive bail shall not be required, nor excessive fines imposed, nor cruel and unusual punishments inflicted." We begin with the principle, settled by *Gregg*, that capital punishment is constitutional. It necessarily follows that there must be a means of carrying it out. Some risk of pain is inherent in any method of execution—no matter how humane—if only from the prospect of error in following the required procedure. It is clear, then, that the Constitution does not demand the avoidance of all risk of pain in carrying out executions.

Petitioners do not claim that it does. Rather, they contend that the Eighth Amendment prohibits procedures that create an "unnecessary risk" of pain. Specifically, they argue that courts must evaluate "(a) the severity of pain risked, (b) the likelihood of that pain occurring, and (c) the extent to which alternative means are feasible, either by modifying existing execution procedures or adopting alternative procedures." Petitioners envision that the quantum of risk necessary to make out an Eighth Amendment claim will vary according to the severity of the pain and the availability of alternatives, but that the risk must be "significant" to trigger Eighth Amendment scrutiny.

Kentucky responds that this "unnecessary risk" standard is tantamount to a requirement that States adopt the "'least risk'" alternative in carrying out an execution, a standard the Commonwealth contends will cast recurring constitutional doubt on any procedure adopted by the States. Instead, Kentucky urges the Court to approve the "'substantial risk'" test used by the courts below.

This Court has never invalidated a State's chosen procedure for carrying out a sentence of death as the infliction of cruel and unusual punishment. In *Wilkerson v. Utah*, 99 U.S. 130 (1879), we upheld a sentence to death by firing squad imposed by a territorial court, rejecting the argument that such a sentence constituted cruel and unusual punishment. We noted there the difficulty of "defin[ing] with exactness the extent of the constitutional provision which provides that cruel and unusual punishments shall not be inflicted." Rather than undertake such an effort, the *Wilkerson* Court simply noted that "it is safe to affirm that punishments of torture, . . . and all others in the same line of unnecessary cruelty, are forbidden" by the Eighth Amendment. . . .

We carried these principles further in *In re Kemmler*, 136 U.S. 436 (1890). There we rejected an opportunity to incorporate the Eighth Amendment against the States in a challenge to the first execution by electrocution, to be carried out by the State of New York. In passing over that question, however, we observed that "[p]unishments are cruel when they involve torture or a lingering death; but the punishment of death is not cruel within the meaning of that word as used in the Constitution. It implies there something inhuman and barbarous, something more than the mere extinguishment of life." We noted that the New York statute adopting electrocution as a method of execution "was passed in the effort to devise a more humane method of reaching the result."

Petitioners do not claim that lethal injection or the proper administration of the particular protocol adopted by Kentucky by themselves constitute the cruel or wanton infliction of pain. Quite the contrary, they concede that "if performed properly," an execution carried out under Kentucky's procedures would be "humane and constitutional." . . . Instead, petitioners claim that there is a significant risk that the procedures will not be properly followed—in particular, that the sodium thiopental will not be properly administered to achieve its intended effect—resulting in severe pain when the other chemicals are administered. . . .

Simply because an execution method may result in pain, either by accident or as an inescapable consequence of death, does not establish the sort of "objectively intolerable risk of harm" that qualifies as cruel and unusual. In

Louisiana ex rel. Francis v. Resweber, 329 U.S. 459 (1947), a plurality of the Court upheld a second attempt at executing a prisoner by electrocution after a mechanical malfunction had interfered with the first attempt. The principal opinion noted that "[a]ccidents happen for which no man is to blame," and concluded that such "an accident, with no suggestion of malevolence," did not give rise to an Eighth Amendment violation.

As Justice FRANKFURTER noted in a separate opinion based on the Due Process Clause, however, "a hypothetical situation" involving "a series of abortive attempts at electrocution" would present a different case. In terms of our present Eighth Amendment analysis, such a situation—unlike an "innocent misadventure"—would demonstrate an "objectively intolerable risk of harm" that officials may not ignore. In other words, an isolated mishap alone does not give rise to an Eighth Amendment violation, precisely because such an event, while regrettable, does not suggest cruelty, or that the procedure at issue gives rise to a "substantial risk of serious harm." . . .

Petitioners contend that there is a risk of improper administration of thiopental because the doses are difficult to mix into solution form and load into syringes; because the protocol fails to establish a rate of injection, which could lead to a failure of the IV; because it is possible that the IV catheters will infiltrate into surrounding tissue, causing an inadequate dose to be delivered to the vein; because of inadequate facilities and training; and because Kentucky has no reliable means of monitoring the anesthetic depth of the prisoner after the sodium thiopental has been administered.

As for the risk that the sodium thiopental would be improperly prepared, petitioners contend that Kentucky employs untrained personnel who are unqualified to calculate and mix an adequate dose, especially in light of the omission of volume and concentration amounts from the written protocol. The state trial court, however, specifically found that "[i]f the manufacturers' instructions for reconstitution of Sodium Thiopental are followed, . . . there would be minimal risk of improper mixing, despite converse testimony that a layperson would have difficulty performing this task." We cannot say that this finding is clearly erroneous, particularly when that finding is substantiated by expert testimony. . . .

Likewise, the asserted problems related to the IV lines do not establish a sufficiently substantial risk of harm to meet the requirements of the Eighth Amendment. Kentucky has put in place several important safeguards to ensure that an adequate dose of sodium thiopental is delivered to the condemned prisoner. The most significant of these is the written protocol's requirement that members of the IV team must have at least one year of professional experience as a certified medical assistant, phlebotomist, EMT, paramedic, or military corpsman. . . .

In addition, the presence of the warden and deputy warden in the execution chamber with the prisoner allows them to watch for signs of IV problems, including infiltration. . . .

The dissent believes that rough-and-ready tests for checking consciousness—calling the inmate's name, brushing his eyelashes, or presenting him with strong, noxious odors—could materially decrease the risk of administering the second and third drugs before the sodium thiopental has taken effect. Again, the risk at issue is already attenuated, given the steps Kentucky has taken to ensure the proper administration of the first drug. Moreover, the scenario the dissent posits involves a level of unconsciousness allegedly sufficient to avoid detection of improper administration of the anesthesia under Kentucky's procedure, but not sufficient to prevent pain. There is no indication that the basic tests the dissent advocates can make such fine distinctions. If these tests are effective only in determining whether the sodium thiopental has entered the inmate's bloodstream, the record confirms that the visual inspection of the IV site under Kentucky's procedure achieves that objective.

The dissent would continue the stay of these executions (and presumably the many others held in abeyance pending decision in this case) and send the case back to the lower courts to determine whether such added measures redress an "untoward" risk of pain. But an inmate cannot succeed on an Eighth Amendment claim simply by showing one more step the State could take as a failsafe for other, independently adequate measures. This approach would serve no meaningful purpose and would frustrate the State's legitimate interest in carrying out a sentence of death in a timely manner.

Reasonable people of good faith disagree on the morality and efficacy of capital punishment, and for many who oppose it, no method of execution would ever be acceptable. But as Justice FRANKFURTER stressed in Resweber, "[o]ne must be on guard against finding in personal disapproval a reflection of more or less prevailing condemnation." This Court has ruled that capital punishment is not prohibited under our Constitution, and that the States may enact laws specifying that sanction. "[T]he power of a State to pass laws means little if the State cannot enforce them." *McCleskey v. Zant*, 499 U.S. 467 (1991).

Kentucky has adopted a method of execution believed to be the most humane available, one it shares with 35 other States. Petitioners agree that, if administered as intended, that procedure will result in a painless death. The risks of maladministration they have suggested—such as improper mixing of chemicals and improper setting of IVs by trained and experienced personnel—cannot remotely be characterized as "objectively intolerable." . . .

Throughout our history, whenever a method of execution has been challenged in this Court as cruel and unusual, the Court has rejected the challenge. Our society has nonetheless steadily moved to more humane methods of carrying out capital punishment. The firing squad, hanging, the electric chair, and the gas chamber have each in turn given way to more humane methods, culminating in today's consensus on lethal injection. The broad framework of the Eighth Amendment has accommodated this progress toward more humane methods of execution, and our approval of a particular method in the past has not precluded legislatures from taking the steps they deem appropriate, in light of new developments, to ensure humane capital punishment. There is no reason to suppose that today's decision will be any different.

The judgment below concluding that Kentucky's procedure is consistent with the Eighth Amendment is, accordingly, affirmed.

☐ *Justice ALITO, concurring.*

I join the plurality opinion but write separately to explain my view of how the holding should be implemented. The opinion concludes that "a State's refusal to change its method [of execution] can be viewed as 'cruel and unusual' under the Eighth Amendment" if the State, "without a legitimate penological justification," rejects an alternative method that is "feasible" and "readily" available and that would "significantly reduce a substantial risk of severe pain." Properly understood, this standard will not, as Justice THOMAS predicts, lead to litigation that enables "those seeking to abolish the death penalty . . . to embroil the States in never-ending litigation concerning the adequacy of their execution procedures." . . .

☐ *Justice BREYER, concurring in the judgment.*

Assuming the lawfulness of the death penalty itself, petitioners argue that Kentucky's method of execution, lethal injection, nonetheless constitutes a constitutionally forbidden, "cruel and usual punishmen[t]." In respect to how a court should review such a claim, I agree with Justice GINSBURG. She highlights the relevant question, whether the method creates an untoward, readily avoidable risk of inflicting severe and unnecessary suffering. I agree that the relevant factors—the "degree of risk," the "magnitude of pain," and the "availability of alternatives"—are interrelated and each must be considered. At the same time, I believe that the legal merits of the kind of claim presented must inevitably turn not so much upon the wording of an intermediate standard of review as upon facts and evidence. And I cannot find, either in the record in this case or in the literature on the subject, sufficient evidence that Kentucky's execution method poses the "significant and unnecessary risk of inflicting severe pain" that petitioners assert. . . .

☐ *Justice STEVENS, concurring in the judgment.*

When we granted *certiorari* in this case, I assumed that our decision would bring the debate about lethal injection as a method of execution to a close. It now seems clear that it will not. The question whether a similar three-drug protocol may be used in other States remains open, and may well be answered differently in a future case on the basis of a more complete record. Instead of ending the controversy, I am now convinced that this case will generate debate not only about the constitutionality of the three-drug protocol, and specifically about the justification for the use of the paralytic agent, pancuronium bromide, but also about the justification for the death penalty itself. . . .

In *Gregg v. Georgia*, 428 U.S. 153 (1976), we explained that unless a criminal sanction serves a legitimate penological function, it constitutes "gratuitous infliction of suffering" in violation of the Eighth Amendment. We then identified three societal purposes for death as a sanction: incapacitation, deterrence, and retribution (joint opinion of STEWART, POWELL, and STEVENS, JJ.). In the past three decades, however, each of these rationales has been called into question.

While incapacitation may have been a legitimate rationale in 1976, the recent rise in statutes providing for life imprisonment without the possibility of parole demonstrates that incapacitation is neither a necessary nor a sufficient justification for the death penalty. Moreover, a recent poll indicates that support for the death penalty drops significantly when life without the possibility of parole is presented as an alternative option. And the available sociological evidence suggests that juries are less likely to impose the death penalty when life without parole is available as a sentence.

The legitimacy of deterrence as an acceptable justification for the death penalty is also questionable, at best. Despite 30 years of empirical research in the area, there remains no reliable statistical evidence that capital punishment in fact deters potential offenders. In the absence of such evidence, deterrence cannot serve as a sufficient penological justification for this uniquely severe and irrevocable punishment.

We are left, then, with retribution as the primary rationale for imposing the death penalty. And indeed, it is the retribution rationale that animates much of the remaining enthusiasm for the death penalty. Our Eighth Amendment jurisprudence has narrowed the class of offenders eligible for the death penalty to include only those who have committed outrageous crimes defined by specific aggravating factors. It is the cruel treatment of victims that provides the most persuasive arguments for prosecutors seeking the death penalty. A natural response to such heinous crimes is a thirst for vengeance.

At the same time, however, as the thoughtful opinions by THE CHIEF JUSTICE and Justice GINSBURG make pellucidly clear, our society has moved away from public and painful retribution towards ever more humane forms of punishment. State-sanctioned killing is therefore becoming more and more anachronistic. In an attempt to bring executions in line with our evolving standards of decency, we have adopted increasingly less painful methods of execution, and then declared previous methods barbaric and archaic. But by requiring that an execution be relatively painless, we necessarily protect the inmate from enduring any punishment that is comparable to the suffering inflicted on his victim. This trend, while appropriate and required by the Eighth Amendment's prohibition on cruel and unusual punishment, actually undermines the very premise on which public approval of the retribution rationale is based. . . .

Our decisions in 1976 upholding the constitutionality of the death penalty relied heavily on our belief that adequate procedures were in place that would avoid the danger of discriminatory application identified by Justice DOUGLAS' opinion in *Furman*, of arbitrary application identified by Justice STEWART, and of excessiveness identified by Justices BRENNAN and MARSHALL. In subsequent years a number of our decisions relied on the premise that "death is different" from every other form of punishment to justify rules minimizing the risk of error in capital cases. Ironically, however, more recent cases have endorsed procedures that provide less protections to capital defendants than to ordinary offenders. . . .

In sum, just as Justice WHITE ultimately based his conclusion in *Furman* on his extensive exposure to countless cases for which death is the authorized penalty, I have relied on my own experience in reaching the conclusion that the imposition of the death penalty represents "the pointless and needless extinction of life with only marginal contributions to any discernible social or public purposes. A penalty with such negligible returns to the State [is] patently excessive and cruel and unusual punishment violative of the Eighth Amendment."

The conclusion that I have reached with regard to the constitutionality of the death penalty itself makes my decision in this case particularly difficult. It does not, however, justify a refusal to respect precedents that remain a part of our law. This Court has held that the death penalty is constitutional, and has established a framework for evaluating the constitutionality of particular methods of execution. Under those precedents, whether as interpreted by THE CHIEF JUSTICE or Justice GINSBURG, I am persuaded that the evidence adduced by petitioners fails to prove that Kentucky's lethal injection protocol violates the Eighth Amendment. Accordingly, I join the Court's judgment.

☐ *Justice SCALIA, with whom Justice THOMAS joins, concurring in the judgment.*

I join the opinion of Justice THOMAS concurring in the judgment. I write separately to provide what I think is needed response to Justice STEVENS' separate opinion.

Justice STEVENS concludes as follows: "[T]he imposition of the death penalty represents the pointless and needless extinction of life with only marginal contributions to any discernible social or public purposes. A penalty with such negligble returns to the State [is] patently excessive and cruel and unusual punishment violative of the Eighth Amendment."

This conclusion is insupportable as an interpretation of the Constitution, which generally leaves it to democratically elected legislatures rather than courts to decide what makes significant contribution to social or public purposes. Besides that more general proposition, the very text of the document recognizes that the death penalty is a permissible legislative choice. The Fifth Amendment expressly requires a presentment or indictment of a grand jury to hold a person to answer for "a capital, or otherwise infamous crime," and prohibits deprivation of "life" without due process of law. The same Congress that proposed the Eighth Amendment also enacted the Act of April 30, 1790, which made several offenses punishable by death. There is simply no legal authority for the proposition that the imposition of death as a criminal penalty is unconstitutional other than the opinions in *Furman v. Georgia*, 408 U.S. 238 (1972), which established a nationwide moratorium on capital punishment that Justice STEVENS had a hand in ending four years later in *Gregg*. . . .

According to Justice STEVENS, the death penalty promotes none of the purposes of criminal punishment because it neither prevents more crimes than alternative measures nor serves a retributive purpose. He argues that "the recent rise in statutes providing for life imprisonment without the possibility of parole" means that States have a ready alternative to the death penalty. Taking the points together, Justice STEVENS concludes that the availability of alternatives, and what he describes as the unavailability of "reliable statistical evidence," renders capital punishment unconstitutional. In his view, the benefits of capital punishment—as compared to other forms of punishment such as life imprisonment—are outweighed by the costs.

These conclusions are not supported by the available data. Justice STEVENS' analysis barely acknowledges the "significant body of recent evidence that capital punishment may well have a deterrent effect, possibly a quite powerful one." . . .

But even if Justice STEVENS' assertion about the deterrent value of the death penalty were correct, the death penalty would yet be constitutional (as he concedes) if it served the appropriate purpose of retribution. I would think it difficult indeed to prove that a criminal sanction fails to serve a retributive purpose—a judgment that strikes me as inherently subjective and insusceptible of judicial review. Justice STEVENS, however, concludes that, because the Eighth Amendment "protect[s] the inmate from enduring any punishment that is comparable to the suffering inflicted on his victim," capital punishment serves no retributive purpose at all. The infliction of any pain, according to Justice STEVENS, violates the Eighth Amendment's prohibition against cruel and unusual punishments, but so too does the imposition of capital punishment without pain because a criminal penalty lacks a retributive purpose unless it inflicts pain commensurate with the pain that the criminal has caused. In other words, if a punishment is not retributive enough, it is not retributive at all. To state this proposition is to refute it, as Justice STEVENS once understood. "[T]he decision that capital punishment may be the appropriate sanction in extreme cases is an expression of the community's belief that certain crimes are themselves so grievous an affront to humanity that the only adequate response may be the penalty of death." *Gregg*.

Justice STEVENS' final refuge in his cost-benefit analysis is a familiar one: There is a risk that an innocent person might be convicted and sentenced to death—though not a risk that Justice STEVENS can quantify, because he lacks a single example of a person executed for a crime he did not commit in the current American system. His analysis of this risk is thus a series of sweeping condemnations that, if taken seriously, would prevent any punishment under any criminal justice system. . . .

But of all Justice STEVENS' criticisms of the death penalty, the hardest to take is his bemoaning of "the enormous costs that death penalty litigation imposes on society," including the "burden on the courts and the lack of finality for victim's families." Those costs, those burdens, and that lack of finality are in large measure the creation of Justice STEVENS and other Justices opposed to the death penalty, who have "encumber[ed] [it] . . . with unwarranted restrictions neither contained in the text of the Constitution nor reflected in two centuries of practice under it"—the product of their policy views "not shared by the vast majority of the American people."

But actually none of this really matters. As Justice STEVENS explains, "'objective evidence, though of great importance, [does] not wholly determine the controversy, for the Constitution contemplates that in the end our own judgment will be brought to bear on the question of the acceptability of the death penalty under the Eighth Amendment.'" "I have relied on my own experience in reaching the conclusion that the imposition of the death penalty" is unconstitutional.

Purer expression cannot be found of the principle of rule by judicial fiat. In the face of Justice STEVENS' experience, the experience of all others is, it appears, of little consequence. The experience of the state legislatures and the Congress—who retain the death penalty as a form of punishment—is dismissed as "the product of habit and inattention rather than an acceptable deliberative process." The experience of social scientists whose studies indicate that the death penalty deters crime is relegated to a footnote. The experience of fellow citizens who support the death penalty is described, with only the most thinly veiled condemnation, as stemming from a "thirst for vengeance." It is Justice STEVENS' experience that reigns over all.

I take no position on the desirability of the death penalty, except to say that its value is eminently debatable and the subject of deeply, indeed passionately, held views—which means, to me, that it is preeminently not a matter to be resolved here. And especially not when it is explicitly permitted by the Constitution.

☐ *Justice THOMAS, with whom Justice SCALIA joins, concurring in the judgment.*

Although I agree that petitioners have failed to establish that Kentucky's lethal injection protocol violates the Eighth Amendment, I write separately because I cannot subscribe to the plurality opinion's formulation of the governing standard. As I understand it, that opinion would hold that a method of execution violates the Eighth Amendment if it poses a substantial risk of severe pain that could be significantly reduced by adopting readily available alternative procedures. This standard—along with petitioners' proposed "unnecessary risk" standard and the dissent's "untoward risk" standard—finds no support in the original understanding of the Cruel and Unusual Punishments Clause or in our previous method-of-execution cases; casts constitutional doubt on long-accepted methods of execution; and injects the Court into matters it has no institutional capacity to resolve. Because, in my view, a method of execution violates the Eighth Amendment only if it is deliberately designed to inflict pain, I concur only in the judgment.

The Eighth Amendment's prohibition on the "inflict[ion]" of "cruel and unusual punishments" must be understood in light of the historical practices that led the Framers to include it in the Bill of Rights. . . .

That the Constitution permits capital punishment in principle does not, of course, mean that all methods of execution are constitutional. In English and early colonial practice, the death penalty was not a uniform punishment, but rather a range of punishments, some of which the Framers likely regarded as cruel and unusual. Death by hanging was the most common mode of execution both before and after 1791, and there is no doubt that it remained a permissible punishment after enactment of the Eighth Amendment. In addition to hanging, which was intended to, and often did, result in a quick and painless death, "[o]fficials also wielded a set of tools capable of intensifying a death sentence," that is, "ways of producing a punishment worse than death."

One such "tool" was burning at the stake. Because burning, unlike hanging, was always painful and destroyed the body, it was considered "a form of super-capital punishment, worse than death itself." Reserved for offenders whose crimes were thought to pose an especially grave threat to the social order—such as slaves who killed their masters and women who killed their husbands—burning a person alive was so dreadful a punishment that sheriffs sometimes hanged the offender first "as an act of charity." Other methods of intensifying a death sentence included "gibbeting," or hanging the condemned in an iron cage so that his body would decompose in public view, and "public dissection," a punishment Blackstone associated with murder, 4 W. Blackstone, *Commentaries* (1769). But none of these was the worst fate a criminal could meet. That was reserved for the most dangerous and reprobate offenders—traitors. "The punishment of high treason," Blackstone wrote, was "very solemn and terrible," and involved "embowelling alive, beheading, and quartering." . . .

The principal object of these aggravated forms of capital punishment was to terrorize the criminal, and thereby more effectively deter the crime. Their defining characteristic was that they were purposely designed to inflict pain and suffering beyond that necessary to cause death. These "superadded" circumstances "were carefully handed out to apply terror where it was thought to be most needed," and were designed "to ensure that death would be slow and painful, and thus all the more frightening to contemplate."

Although the Eighth Amendment was not the subject of extensive discussion during the debates on the Bill of Rights, there is good reason to believe that the Framers viewed such enhancements to the death penalty as falling within the prohibition of the Cruel and Unusual Punishments Clause.

Moreover, the evidence we do have from the debates on the Constitution confirms that the Eighth Amendment was intended to disable Congress from imposing torturous punishments. . . .

Consistent with the original understanding of the Cruel and Unusual Punishments Clause, this Court's cases have repeatedly taken the view that the Framers intended to prohibit torturous modes of punishment akin to those that formed the historical backdrop of the Eighth Amendment. . . .

In the first case, *Wilkerson v. Utah*, 99 U.S. 130 (1879), the Court rejected the contention that death by firing squad was cruel and unusual. . . . Similarly, when the Court in *In re Kemmler*, 136 U.S. 436 (1890), unanimously rejected a challenge to electrocution, it interpreted the Eighth Amendment to prohibit punishments that "were manifestly cruel and unusual, as burning at the stake, crucifixion, breaking on the wheel, or the like." . . . Finally, in *Louisiana ex rel. Francis v. Resweber*, 329 U.S. 459 (1947), the Court rejected the petitioner's contention that the Eighth Amendment prohibited Louisiana from subjecting him to a second attempt at electrocution, the first attempt having failed when "[t]he executioner threw the switch but, presumably because of some mechanical difficulty, death did not result." . . .

We have never suggested that a method of execution is "cruel and unusual" within the meaning of the Eighth Amendment simply because it involves a risk of pain—whether "substantial," "unnecessary," or "untoward"—that could be reduced by adopting alternative procedures. And for good reason. It strains credulity to suggest that the defining characteristic of burning at the stake, disemboweling, drawing and quartering, beheading, and the like was that they involved risks of pain that could be eliminated by using alternative methods of execution. Quite plainly, what defined these punishments was that they were designed to inflict torture as a way of enhancing a death sentence; they were intended to produce a penalty worse than death, to accomplish something "more than the mere extinguishment of life." The evil the Eighth Amendment targets is intentional infliction of gratuitous pain, and that is the standard our method-of-execution cases have explicitly or implicitly invoked. . . .

In short, I reject as both unprecedented and unworkable any standard that would require the courts to weigh the relative advantages and disadvantages of different methods of execution or of different procedures for implementing a given method of execution. To the extent that there is any comparative element to the inquiry, it should be limited to whether the challenged method inherently inflicts significantly more pain than traditional modes of execution such as hanging and the firing squad.

Judged under the proper standard, this is an easy case. It is undisputed that Kentucky adopted its lethal injection protocol in an effort to make capital punishment more humane, not to add elements of terror, pain, or disgrace to the death penalty. And it is undisputed that, if administered properly, Kentucky's lethal injection protocol will result in a swift and painless death. As the Sixth Circuit observed in rejecting a similar challenge to Tennessee's lethal injection protocol, we "do not have a situation where the State has any intent (or anything approaching intent) to inflict unnecessary pain; the complaint is that the State's pain-avoidance procedure may fail because the executioners may make a mistake in implementing it." But "[t]he risk of negligence in implementing a death-penalty procedure . . . does not establish a cognizable Eighth Amendment claim." Because Kentucky's lethal injection protocol is designed to eliminate pain rather than to inflict it, petitioners' challenge must fail. I accordingly concur in the Court's judgment affirming the decision below.

☐ *Justice GINSBURG, with whom Justice SOUTER joins, dissenting.*

It is undisputed that the second and third drugs used in Kentucky's three-drug lethal injection protocol, pancuronium bromide and potassium chloride, would cause a conscious inmate to suffer excruciating pain. Pancuronium bromide paralyzes the lung muscles and results in slow asphyxiation. Potassium chloride causes burning and intense pain as it circulates throughout the body. Use of pancuronium bromide and potassium chloride on a conscious inmate, the plurality recognizes, would be "constitutionally unacceptable."

The constitutionality of Kentucky's protocol therefore turns on whether inmates are adequately anesthetized by the first drug in the protocol, sodium thiopental. Kentucky's system is constitutional, the plurality states, because "petitioners have not shown that the risk of an inadequate dose of the first drug is substantial." I would not dispose of the case so swiftly given the character of the risk at stake. Kentucky's protocol lacks basic safeguards used by other States to confirm that an inmate is unconscious before injection of the second and third drugs. I would vacate and remand with instructions to consider whether Kentucky's omission of those safeguards poses an untoward, readily avoidable risk of inflicting severe and unnecessary pain.

The Court has considered the constitutionality of a specific method of execution on only three prior occasions. Those cases, and other decisions cited by the parties and *amici*, provide little guidance on the standard that should govern petitioners' challenge to Kentucky's lethal injection protocol [*Wilkerson, Kemmler, Resweber*]. . . . No clear standard for determining the constitutionality of a method of execution emerges from these decisions. Moreover, the age of the opinions limits their utility as an aid to resolution of the present controversy. The Eighth Amendment, we have held, " 'must draw its meaning from the evolving standards of decency that mark the progress of a maturing society.' " *Atkins v. Virginia*, 536 U.S. 304 (2002) (quoting *Trop v. Dulles*, 356 U.S. 86 (1958). *Wilkerson* was decided 129 years ago, *Kemmler* 118 years ago, and *Resweber* 61 years ago. Whatever little light our prior method-of-execution cases might shed is thus dimmed by the passage of time.

Further phrases and tests can be drawn from more recent decisions, for example, *Gregg v. Georgia*, 428 U.S. 153 (1976). Speaking of capital punishment in the abstract, the lead opinion said that the Eighth Amendment prohibits "the unnecessary and wanton infliction of pain"; the same opinion also cautioned that a death sentence cannot "be imposed under sentencing procedures that creat[e] a substantial risk that it would be inflicted in an arbitrary and capricious manner." . . .

Other than using qualified and trained personnel to establish IV access, however, Kentucky does little to ensure that the inmate receives an effective dose of sodium thiopental. After siting the catheters, the IV team leaves the execution chamber. From that point forward, only the warden and deputy warden remain with the inmate. Neither the warden nor the deputy warden has any medical training.

The warden relies on visual observation to determine whether the inmate "appears" unconscious. In Kentucky's only previous execution by lethal injection, the warden's position allowed him to see the inmate best from the waist down, with only a peripheral view of the inmate's face. No other check for consciousness occurs before injection of pancuronium bromide. . . .

Nor does Kentucky monitor the effectiveness of the sodium thiopental using readily available equipment, even though the inmate is already connected to an electrocardiogram (EKG). . . .

Recognizing the importance of a window between the first and second drugs, other States have adopted safeguards not contained in Kentucky's protocol. . . . In California, a member of the IV team brushes the inmate's eyelashes, speaks to him, and shakes him at the halfway point and, again, at the completion of the sodium thiopental injection. In Alabama, a member of the execution team "begin[s] by saying the condemned inmate's name. If there is no response, the team member will gently stroke the condemned inmate's eyelashes. If there is no response, the team member will then pinch the condemned inmate's arm." In Indiana, officials inspect the injection site after administration of sodium thiopental, say the inmate's name, touch him, and use ammonia tablets to test his response to a noxious nasal stimulus.

These checks provide a degree of assurance—missing from Kentucky's protocol—that the first drug has been properly administered. They are simple and essentially costless to employ, yet work to lower the risk that the inmate will be subjected to the agony of conscious suffocation caused by pancuronium bromide and the searing pain caused by potassium chloride. The record contains no explanation why Kentucky does not take any of these elementary measures. . . .

"The easiest and most obvious way to ensure that an inmate is unconscious during an execution," petitioners argued to the Kentucky Supreme Court, "is to check for consciousness prior to injecting pancuronium [bromide]." The court did not address petitioners' argument. I would therefore remand with instructions to consider whether the failure to include readily available safeguards to confirm that the inmate is unconscious after injection of sodium thiopental, in combination with the other elements of Kentucky's protocol, creates an untoward, readily avoidable risk of inflicting severe and unnecessary pain.

Kennedy v. Louisiana
128 S.CT. 2641 (2008)

In 1995 Louisiana extended the death penalty to the crime of rape of a child under the age of twelve. Five other states—Georgia, Montana, Oklahoma, South Carolina, and Texas—followed, though they required that defendants have a prior rape conviction or other aggravating factor for imposing the death penalty. In 2003 Patrick Kennedy was convicted and sentenced to death for raping his eight-year-old stepdaughter. The state supreme court affirmed and Kennedy appealed that decision.

The state supreme court's decision was reversed by a five-to-four vote. Justice Kennedy delivered the opinion of the Court. Justice Alito filed a dissenting opinion, which Chief Justice Roberts and Justices Scalia and Thomas joined.

☐ *Justice KENNEDY delivered the opinion of the Court.*

The Eighth Amendment, applicable to the States through the Fourteenth Amendment, provides that "[e]xcessive bail shall not be required, nor excessive fines imposed, nor cruel and unusual punishments inflicted." The Amendment proscribes "all excessive punishments, as well as cruel and unusual punishments that may or may not be excessive." *Atkins* [*v. Virginia*, 536 U.S. 304 (2002)]. The Court explained in *Atkins*, and *Roper* [*v. Simmons*, 543 U.S. 551 (2005)], that the Eighth Amendment's protection against excessive or cruel and unusual punishments flows from the basic "precept of justice that punishment for [a] crime should be graduated and proportioned to [the] offense." *Weems v. United States*, 217 U.S. 349 (1910). Whether this requirement has been fulfilled is determined not by the standards that prevailed when the Eighth Amendment was adopted in 1791 but by the norms that "currently prevail." The Amendment "draw[s] its meaning from the evolving standards of decency that mark the progress of a maturing society." *Trop v. Dulles*, 356 U.S. 86 (1958). This is because "[t]he standard of extreme cruelty is not merely descriptive, but necessarily embodies a moral judgment. The standard itself remains the same, but its applicability must change as the basic mores of society change." *Furman v. Georgia*, 408 U.S. 238 (1972).

Evolving standards of decency must embrace and express respect for the dignity of the person, and the punishment of criminals must conform to that rule. As we shall discuss, punishment is justified under one or more of three principal rationales: rehabilitation, deterrence, and retribution. It is the last of these, retribution, that most often can contradict the law's own ends. This is of particular concern when the Court interprets the meaning of the Eighth Amendment in capital cases. When the law punishes by death, it risks its own sudden descent into brutality, transgressing the constitutional commitment to decency and restraint.

For these reasons we have explained that capital punishment must "be limited to those offenders who commit 'a narrow category of the most serious crimes' and whose extreme culpability makes them 'the most deserving of execution.'" *Roper*. Though the death penalty is not invariably unconstitutional, see *Gregg v. Georgia*, 428 U.S. 153 (1976), the Court insists upon confining the instances in which the punishment can be imposed.

Applying this principle, we held in *Roper* and *Atkins* that the execution of juveniles and mentally retarded persons are punishments violative of the Eighth Amendment because the offender had a diminished personal responsibility for the crime. The Court further has held that the death penalty can be disproportionate to the crime itself where the crime did not result, or was not intended to result, in death of the victim. In *Coker*, for instance, the Court held it would be unconstitutional to execute an offender who had raped an adult woman. On the other hand, in *Tison v. Arizona*, 481 U.S. 137 (1987), the Court allowed the defendants' death sentences to stand where they did not themselves kill the victims but their involvement in the events leading up to the murders was active, recklessly indifferent, and substantial.

In these cases the Court has been guided by "objective indicia of society's standards, as expressed in legislative enactments and state practice with respect to executions." The inquiry does not end there, however. Consensus is not dispositive. Whether the death penalty is disproportionate to the crime committed depends as well upon the standards elaborated by controlling precedents and by the Court's own understanding and interpretation of the Eighth Amendment's text, history, meaning, and purpose.

Based both on consensus and our own independent judgment, our holding is that a death sentence for one who raped but did not kill a child, and who did not intend to assist another in killing the child, is unconstitutional under the Eighth and Fourteenth Amendments.

The existence of objective indicia of consensus against making a crime punishable by death was a relevant concern in *Roper, Atkins, Coker* [*v. Georgia*, 433 U.S. 584 (1997)], and *Enmund* [*v. Florida*, 458 U.S. 782 (1982)], and we follow the approach of those cases here. The history of the death penalty for the crime of rape is an instructive beginning point.

In 1925, 18 States, the District of Columbia, and the Federal Government had statutes that authorized the death penalty for the rape of a child or an adult. Between 1930 and 1964, 455 people were executed for those crimes.

In 1972, *Furman* invalidated most of the state statutes authorizing the death penalty for the crime of rape; and in Furman's aftermath only six States reenacted their capital rape provisions. Three States—Georgia, North Carolina, and Louisiana—did so with respect to all rape offenses. Three States—Florida, Mississippi, and Tennessee—did so with respect only to child rape. Louisiana reintroduced the death penalty for rape of a child in 1995. Under the current statute, any anal, vaginal, or oral intercourse with a child under the age of 13 constitutes aggravated rape and is punishable by death. Mistake of age is not a defense, so the statute imposes strict liability in this regard. Five States have since followed Louisiana's lead: Georgia, Montana, Oklahoma, South Carolina, and Texas. Four of these States' statutes are more narrow than Louisiana's in that only offenders with a previous rape conviction are death eligible.

By contrast, 44 States have not made child rape a capital offense. As for federal law, Congress in the Federal Death Penalty Act of 1994 expanded the number of federal crimes for which the death penalty is a permissible sentence, including certain nonhomicide offenses; but it did not do the same for child rape or abuse. . . .

Definitive resolution of state-law issues is for the States' own courts, and there may be disagreement over the statistics. It is further true that some States, including States that have addressed the issue in just the last few years, have made child rape a capital offense. The summary recited here, however, does allow us to make certain comparisons with the data cited in the *Atkins*, *Roper*, and *Enmund* cases.

When *Atkins* was decided in 2002, 30 States, including 12 noncapital jurisdictions, prohibited the death penalty for mentally retarded offenders; 20 permitted it. When *Roper* was decided in 2005, the numbers disclosed a similar division among the States: 30 States prohibited the death penalty for juveniles, 18 of which permitted the death penalty for other offenders; and 20 States authorized it. Both in *Atkins* and in *Roper*, we noted that the practice of executing mentally retarded and juvenile offenders was infrequent. Only five States had executed an offender known to have an IQ below 70 between 1989 and 2002, and only three States had executed a juvenile offender between 1995 and 2005.

The statistics in *Enmund* bear an even greater similarity to the instant case. There eight jurisdictions had authorized imposition of the death penalty solely for participation in a robbery during which an accomplice committed murder, and six defendants between 1954 and 1982 had been sentenced to death for felony murder where the defendant did not personally commit the homicidal assault. These facts, the Court concluded, "weigh[ed] on the side of rejecting capital punishment for the crime."

The evidence of a national consensus with respect to the death penalty for child rapists, as with respect to juveniles, mentally retarded offenders, and vicarious felony murderers, shows divided opinion but, on balance, an opinion against it. Thirty-seven jurisdictions—36 States plus the Federal Government—have the death penalty. As mentioned above, only six of those jurisdictions authorize the death penalty for rape of a child. Though our review of national consensus is not confined to tallying the number of States with applicable death penalty legislation, it is of significance that, in 45 jurisdictions, petitioner could not be executed for child rape of any kind. That number surpasses the 30 States in *Atkins* and *Roper* and the 42 States in *Enmund* that prohibited the death penalty under the circumstances those cases considered. . . .

We conclude on the basis of this review that there is no clear indication that state legislatures have misinterpreted *Coker* to hold that the death penalty for child rape is unconstitutional. The small number of States that have enacted this penalty, then, is relevant to determining whether there is a consensus against capital punishment for this crime. . . .

There are measures of consensus other than legislation. Statistics about the number of executions may inform the consideration whether capital punishment for the crime of child rape is regarded as unacceptable in our society. These statistics confirm our determination from our review of state statutes that there is a social consensus against the death penalty for the crime of child rape.

Nine States—Florida, Georgia, Louisiana, Mississippi, Montana, Oklahoma, South Carolina, Tennessee, and Texas—have permitted capital punishment for adult or child rape for some length of time between the Court's 1972 decision in *Furman* and today. Yet no individual has been executed for the rape of an adult or child since 1964, and no execution for any other nonhomicide offense has been conducted since 1963.

Louisiana is the only State since 1964 that has sentenced an individual to death for the crime of child rape; and petitioner and Richard Davis, who was convicted and sentenced to death for the aggravated rape of a 5-year-old child by a Louisiana jury in December 2007, are the only two individuals now on death row in the United States for a nonhomicide offense.

After reviewing the authorities informed by contemporary norms, including the history of the death penalty for this and other nonhomicide crimes, current state statutes and new enactments, and the number of executions since 1964, we conclude there is a national consensus against capital punishment for the crime of child rape. As we have said in other Eighth Amendment cases, objective evidence of contemporary values as it relates to punishment for child rape is entitled to great weight, but it does not end our inquiry. "[T]he Constitution contemplates that in the end our own judgment will be brought to bear on the question of the acceptability of the death penalty under the Eighth Amendment." We turn, then, to the resolution of the question before us, which is informed by our precedents and our own understanding of the Constitution and the rights it secures.

It must be acknowledged that there are moral grounds to question a rule barring capital punishment for a crime against an individual that did not result in death. These facts illustrate the point. Here the victim's fright, the sense of betrayal, and the nature of her injuries caused more prolonged physical and mental suffering than, say, a sudden killing by an unseen assassin. The attack was not just on her but on her childhood. For this reason, we should be most reluctant to rely upon the language of the plurality in *Coker*, which posited that, for the victim of rape, "life may not be nearly so happy as it was" but it is not beyond repair. Rape has a permanent psychological, emotional, and sometimes physical impact on the child.

It does not follow, though, that capital punishment is a proportionate penalty for the crime. The constitutional prohibition against excessive or cruel and unusual punishments mandates that the State's power to punish "be exercised within the limits of civilized standards." *Trop.* Evolving standards of decency that mark the progress of a maturing society counsel us to be most hesitant before interpreting the Eighth Amendment to allow the extension of the death penalty, a hesitation that has special force where no life was taken in the commission of the crime. It is an established principle that decency, in its essence, presumes respect for the individual and thus moderation or restraint in the application of capital punishment.

To date the Court has sought to define and implement this principle, for the most part, in cases involving capital murder. One approach has been to insist upon general rules that ensure consistency in determining who receives a death sentence. At the same time the Court has insisted, to ensure restraint and moderation in use of capital punishment, on judging the "character and record of the individual offender and the circumstances of the particular offense as a constitutionally indispensable part of the process of inflicting the penalty of death." *Woodson* [*v. North Carolina*, 428 U.S. 280 (1976)]. . . .

Our response to this case law, which is still in search of a unifying principle, has been to insist upon confining the instances in which capital punishment may be imposed.

Our concern here is limited to crimes against individual persons. We do not address, for example, crimes defining and punishing treason, espionage, terrorism, and drug kingpin activity, which are offenses against the State. As it relates to crimes against individuals, though, the death penalty should not be expanded to instances where the victim's life was not taken. We said in *Coker* of adult rape: "We do not discount the seriousness of rape as a crime. It is highly reprehensible, both in a moral sense and in its almost total contempt for the personal integrity and autonomy of the female victim . . . . Short of homicide, it is the 'ultimate violation of self.' . . . [But] [t]he murderer kills; the rapist, if no more than that, does not. . . . We have the abiding conviction that the death penalty, which 'is unique in its severity and irrevocability,' is an excessive penalty for the rapist who, as such, does not take human life."

The same distinction between homicide and other serious violent offenses against the individual informed the Court's analysis in *Enmund*, where the Court held that the death penalty for the crime of vicarious felony murder is disproportionate to the offense. The Court repeated there the fundamental, moral distinction between a "murderer" and a "robber," noting that while "robbery is a serious crime deserving serious punishment," it is not like death in its "severity and irrevocability."

Consistent with evolving standards of decency and the teachings of our precedents we conclude that, in determining whether the death penalty is excessive, there is a distinction between intentional first-degree murder on the one hand and nonhomicide crimes against individual persons, even including child rape, on the other. The latter crimes may be devastating in their harm, as here, but "in terms of moral depravity and of the injury to the person and to the public," *Coker*, they cannot be compared to murder in their "severity and irrevocability." . . .

Our decision is consistent with the justifications offered for the death penalty. *Gregg* instructs that capital punishment is excessive when it is grossly out of proportion to the crime or it does not fulfill the two distinct social purposes served by the death penalty: retribution and deterrence of capital crimes.

As in *Coker*, here it cannot be said with any certainty that the death penalty for child rape serves no deterrent or retributive function. . . . [Yet, the] incongruity between the crime of child rape and the harshness of the death penalty poses risks of over punishment and counsels against a constitutional ruling that the death penalty can be expanded to include this offense.

The goal of retribution, which reflects society's and the victim's interests in seeing that the offender is repaid for the hurt he caused does not justify the harshness of the death penalty here. In measuring retribution, as well as other objectives of criminal law, it is appropriate to distinguish between a particularly depraved murder that merits death as a form of retribution and the crime of child rape.

There is an additional reason for our conclusion that imposing the death penalty for child rape would not further retributive purposes. . . .

It is not at all evident that the child rape victim's hurt is lessened when the law permits the death of the perpetrator. Capital cases require a long-term commitment by those who testify for the prosecution, especially when guilt and sentencing determinations are in multiple proceedings. In cases like this the key testimony is not just from the family but from the victim herself. During formative years of her adolescence, made all the more daunting for having to come to terms with the brutality of her experience, L. H. was required to discuss the case at length with law enforcement personnel. In a public trial she was required to recount once more all the details of the crime to a jury as the State pursued the death of her stepfather. And in the end the State made L. H. a central figure in its decision to seek the death penalty, telling the jury in closing statements: "[L. H.] is asking you, asking you to set up a time and place when he dies."

Society's desire to inflict the death penalty for child rape by enlisting the child victim to assist it over the course of years in asking for capital punishment forces a moral choice on the child, who is not of mature age to make that choice. The way the death penalty here involves the child victim in its enforcement can compromise a decent legal system; and this is but a subset of fundamental difficulties capital punishment can cause in the administration and enforcement of laws proscribing child rape.

There are, moreover, serious systemic concerns in prosecuting the crime of child rape that are relevant to the constitutionality of making it a capital offense. The problem of unreliable, induced, and even imagined child testimony means there is a "special risk of wrongful execution" in some child rape cases. This undermines, at least to some degree, the meaningful contribution of the death penalty to legitimate goals of punishment. . . .

With respect to deterrence, if the death penalty adds to the risk of non-reporting, that, too, diminishes the penalty's objectives. Underreporting is a common problem with respect to child sexual abuse. Although we know little about what differentiates those who report from those who do not report, one of the most commonly cited reasons for nondisclosure is fear of negative consequences for the perpetrator, a concern that has special force where the abuser is a family member. As a result, punishment by death may not result in more deterrence or more effective enforcement.

In addition, by in effect making the punishment for child rape and murder equivalent, a State that punishes child rape by death may remove a strong incentive for the rapist not to kill the victim. . . . Assuming the offender behaves in a rational way, as one must to justify the penalty on grounds of deterrence, the penalty in some respects gives less protection, not more, to the victim, who is often the sole witness to the crime. It might be argued that, even if the death penalty results in a marginal increase in the incentive to kill, this is counterbalanced by a marginally increased deterrent to commit the crime at all. Whatever balance the legislature strikes, however, uncertainty on the point makes the argument for the penalty less compelling than for homicide crimes. . . .

Our determination that there is a consensus against the death penalty for child rape raises the question whether the Court's own institutional position and its holding will have the effect of blocking further or later consensus in favor of the penalty from developing. The Court, it will be argued, by the act of addressing the constitutionality of the death penalty, intrudes upon the consensus-making process. By imposing a negative restraint, the argument runs, the Court makes it more difficult for consensus to change or emerge. The Court, according to the criticism, itself becomes enmeshed in the process, part judge and part the maker of that which it judges.

These concerns overlook the meaning and full substance of the established proposition that the Eighth Amendment is defined by "the evolving standards of decency that mark the progress of a maturing society." *Trop*. Confirmed by repeated, consistent rulings of this Court, this principle requires that use of the death penalty be restrained. The rule of evolving standards of decency with specific marks on the way to full progress and mature judgment means that resort to the penalty must be reserved for the worst of crimes and limited in its instances of application. In most cases justice is not better served by terminating the life of the perpetrator rather than confining him and preserving the possibility that he and the system will find ways to allow him to understand the enormity of his offense. Difficulties in administering the penalty to ensure against its arbitrary and capricious application require adherence to a rule reserving its use, at this stage of evolving standards and in cases of crimes against individuals, for crimes that take the life of the victim.

The judgment of the Supreme Court of Louisiana upholding the capital sentence is reversed.

☐ *Justice ALITO, with whom THE CHIEF JUSTICE, Justice SCALIA, and Justice THOMAS join, dissenting.*

The Court today holds that the Eighth Amendment categorically prohibits the imposition of the death penalty for the crime of raping a child. This is so, according to the Court, no matter how young the child, no matter how many times the child is raped, no matter how many children the perpetrator rapes, no matter how sadistic the crime, no matter how much physical or psychological trauma is inflicted, and no matter how heinous the perpetrator's prior criminal record may be. The Court provides two reasons for this sweeping conclusion: First, the Court claims to have identified "a national consensus" that the death penalty is never acceptable for the rape of a child; second, the Court concludes, based on its "independent judgment," that imposing the death penalty for child rape is inconsistent with " 'the evolving standards of decency that mark the progress of a maturing society.' " Because neither of these justifications is sound, I respectfully dissent.

I turn first to the Court's claim that there is "a national consensus" that it is never acceptable to impose the death penalty for the rape of a child. The Eighth Amendment's requirements, the Court writes, are "determined not by the standards that prevailed" when the Amendment was adopted but "by the norms that 'currently prevail.' " In assessing current norms, the Court relies primarily on the fact that only 6 of the 50 States now have statutes that permit the death penalty for this offense. But this statistic is a highly unreliable indicator of the views of state lawmakers and their constituents. As I will explain, *dicta* in this Court's decision in *Coker v. Georgia*, 433 U.S. 584 (1977), has stunted legislative consideration of the question whether the death penalty for the targeted offense of raping a young child is consistent with prevailing standards of decency. The *Coker dicta* gave state legislators and others good reason to fear that any law permitting the imposition of the death penalty for this crime would meet precisely the fate that has now befallen the Louisiana statute that is currently before us, and this threat strongly discouraged state legislators—regardless of their own values and those of their constituents—from supporting the enactment of such legislation.

As the Court correctly concludes, the holding in *Coker* was that the Eighth Amendment prohibits the death penalty for the rape of an " 'adult woman,' " and thus *Coker* does not control our decision here. . . .

Because of the effect of the *Coker dicta*, the Court is plainly wrong in comparing the situation here to that in *Atkins* or *Roper v. Simmons*, 543 U.S.

551 (2005). Atkins concerned the constitutionality of imposing the death penalty on a mentally retarded defendant. Thirteen years earlier, in *Penry v. Lynaugh*, 492 U.S. 302 (1989), the Court had held that this was permitted by the Eighth Amendment, and therefore, during the time between *Penry* and *Atkins,* state legislators had reason to believe that this Court would follow its prior precedent and uphold statutes allowing such punishment.

The situation in *Roper* was similar. *Roper* concerned a challenge to the constitutionality of imposing the death penalty on a defendant who had not reached the age of 18 at the time of the crime. Sixteen years earlier in *Stanford v. Kentucky*, 492 U.S. 361 (1989), the Court had rejected a similar challenge, and therefore state lawmakers had cause to believe that laws allowing such punishment would be sustained.

When state lawmakers believe that their decision will prevail on the question whether to permit the death penalty for a particular crime or class of offender, the legislators' resolution of the issue can be interpreted as an expression of their own judgment, informed by whatever weight they attach to the values of their constituents. But when state legislators think that the enactment of a new death penalty law is likely to be futile, inaction cannot reasonably be interpreted as an expression of their understanding of prevailing societal values. In that atmosphere, legislative inaction is more likely to evidence acquiescence.

If anything can be inferred from state legislative developments, the message is very different from the one that the Court perceives. In just the past few years, despite the shadow cast by the *Coker dicta*, five States have enacted targeted capital child-rape laws. If, as the Court seems to think, our society is "[e]volving" toward ever higher "standards of decency," these enactments might represent the beginning of a new evolutionary line.

Such a development would not be out of step with changes in our society's thinking since *Coker* was decided. During that time, reported instances of child abuse have increased dramatically; and there are many indications of growing alarm about the sexual abuse of children. In 1994, Congress enacted the Jacob Wetterling Crimes Against Children and Sexually Violent Offender Registration Program, which requires States receiving certain federal funds to establish registration systems for convicted sex offenders and to notify the public about persons convicted of the sexual abuse of minors. All 50 States have now enacted such statutes. In addition, at least 21 States and the District of Columbia now have statutes permitting the involuntary commitment of sexual predators, and at least 12 States have enacted residency restrictions for sex offenders. . . .

In light of the points discussed above, I believe that the "objective indicia" of our society's "evolving standards of decency" can be fairly summarized as follows. Neither Congress nor juries have done anything that can plausibly be interpreted as evidencing the "national consensus" that the Court perceives. State legislatures, for more than 30 years, have operated under the ominous shadow of the *Coker dicta* and thus have not been free to express their own understanding of our society's standards of decency. And in the months following our grant of certiorari in this case, state legislatures have had an additional reason to pause. Yet despite the inhibiting legal atmosphere that has prevailed since 1977, six States have recently enacted new, targeted child-rape laws.

I do not suggest that six new state laws necessarily establish a "national consensus" or even that they are sure evidence of an ineluctable trend. In terms of the Court's metaphor of moral evolution, these enactments might have turned out to be an evolutionary dead end. But they might also have been the beginning of a strong new evolutionary line. We will never know, because the Court today snuffs out the line in its incipient stage.

The Court is willing to block the potential emergence of a national consensus in favor of permitting the death penalty for child rape because, in the end, what matters is the Court's "own judgment" regarding "the acceptability of the death penalty." Although the Court has much to say on this issue, most of the Court's discussion is not pertinent to the Eighth Amendment question at hand. And once all of the Court's irrelevant arguments are put aside, it is apparent that the Court has provided no coherent explanation for today's decision. . . .

A major theme of the Court's opinion is that permitting the death penalty in child-rape cases is not in the best interests of the victims of these crimes and society at large. In this vein, the Court suggests that it is more painful for child-rape victims to testify when the prosecution is seeking the death penalty. The Court also argues that "a State that punishes child rape by death may remove a strong incentive for the rapist not to kill the victim," and may discourage the reporting of child rape.

These policy arguments, whatever their merits, are simply not pertinent to the question whether the death penalty is "cruel and unusual" punishment. The Eighth Amendment protects the right of an accused. It does not authorize this Court to strike down federal or state criminal laws on the ground that they are not in the best interests of crime victims or the broader society. . . .

The Court also contends that laws permitting the death penalty for the rape of a child create serious procedural problems. Specifically, the Court maintains that it is not feasible to channel the exercise of sentencing discretion in child-rape cases, and that the unreliability of the testimony of child victims creates a danger that innocent defendants will be convicted and executed. Neither of these contentions provides a basis for striking down all capital child-rape laws no matter how carefully and narrowly they are crafted. . . .

After all the arguments noted above are put aside, what is left? What remaining grounds does the Court provide to justify its independent judgment that the death penalty for child rape is categorically unacceptable? I see two.

The first is the proposition that we should be "most hesitant before interpreting the Eighth Amendment to allow the extension of the death penalty." But holding that the Eighth Amendment does not categorically prohibit the death penalty for the rape of a young child would not "extend" or "expand" the death penalty. Laws enacted by the state legislatures are presumptively constitutional, and until today, this Court has not held that capital child rape laws are unconstitutional. Consequently, upholding the constitutionality of such a law would not "extend" or "expand" the death penalty; rather, it would confirm the status of presumptive constitutionality that such laws have enjoyed up to this point. . . .

The Court's final—and, it appears, principal—justification for its holding is that murder, the only crime for which defendants have been executed since this Court's 1976 death penalty decisions, is unique in its moral depravity and in the severity of the injury that it inflicts on the victim and the public. But the Court makes little attempt to defend these conclusions.

With respect to the question of moral depravity, is it really true that every person who is convicted of capital murder and sentenced to death is more morally depraved than every child rapist? Consider the following two cases. In the first, a defendant robs a convenience store and watches as his accomplice shoots the store owner. The defendant acts recklessly, but was not the triggerman and did not intend the killing. See, e.g., *Tison v. Arizona*, 481 U.S. 137 (1987). In the second case, a previously convicted child rapist kidnaps, repeatedly rapes, and tortures multiple child victims. Is it clear that the first defendant is more morally depraved than the second?

The Court's decision here stands in stark contrast to *Atkins* and *Roper*, in which the Court concluded that characteristics of the affected defendants—mental retardation in *Atkins* and youth in *Roper*—diminished their culpability. Nor is this case comparable to *Enmund v. Florida*, 458 U.S. 782 (1982), in which the Court held that the Eighth Amendment prohibits the death penalty where the defendant participated in a robbery during which a murder was committed but did not personally intend for lethal force to be used. I have no doubt that, under the prevailing standards of our society, robbery, the crime that the petitioner in *Enmund* intended to commit, does not evidence the same degree of moral depravity as the brutal rape of a young child. Indeed, I have little doubt that, in the eyes of ordinary Americans, the very worst child rapists—predators who seek out and inflict serious physical and emotional injury on defenseless young children—are the epitome of moral depravity. . . .

In summary, the Court holds that the Eighth Amendment categorically rules out the death penalty in even the most extreme cases of child rape even though: (1) This holding is not supported by the original meaning of the Eighth Amendment; (2) neither *Coker* nor any other prior precedent commands this result; (3) there are no reliable "objective indicia" of a "national consensus" in support of the Court's position; (4) sustaining the constitutionality of the state law before us would not "extend" or "expand" the death penalty; (5) this Court has previously rejected the proposition that the Eighth Amendment is a one-way ratchet that prohibits legislatures from adopting new capital punishment statutes to meet new problems; (6) the worst child rapists exhibit the epitome of moral depravity; and (7) child rape inflicts grievous injury on victims and on society in general.

The party attacking the constitutionality of a state statute bears the "heavy burden" of establishing that the law is unconstitutional. *Gregg*. That burden has not been discharged here, and I would therefore affirm the decision of the Louisiana Supreme Court.

12

THE EQUAL PROTECTION OF THE LAWS

By a six-to-three vote in *Engquist v. Oregon Department of Agriculture*, 128 S.Ct. 2146 (2008), the Court held that government employees who claim that they were singled out for arbitrary, irrational, or vindictive treatment by supervisors may not claim that they are a "class of one" and protected by the equal protection clause; they must claim that their mistreatment was due to discrimination based on race, sex, or another protected category. Writing for the Court, Justice Roberts held that the "class-of-one theory of equal protection" was "simply a poor fit in the public employment context" because government needs "broad discretion" to make "subjective and individualized" decisions about employees. In his words: "To treat employees differently is not to classify them in a way that raises equal protection concerns. . . . A challenge that one has been treated individually in this context, instead of like everyone else, is a challenge to the underlying nature of the governmental action." The chief justice added, "The federal court is not the appropriate forum in which to review the multitude of personnel decisions that are made daily by public agencies." Anup Engquist, a native of India, had experienced problems with laboratory co-workers and management over ten years and was effectively laid off in 2002 after being given the choice to move to another position, for which she was deemed unqualified, or accept a demotion, which she denied to accept. In response, Engquist brought a "class-of-one" equal protection suit, alleging that she dismissed for "arbitrary, vindictive, and malicious reasons," and not because she was a member of an identified class protected by the equal protection clause. Justice Stevens, joined by Justices Souter and Ginsburg, dissented, contending that the majority "carves a novel exception out of state employees' constitutional rights" and that there is a "clear distinction between an exercise of discretion and an arbitrary decision."

C | *Affirmative Action and Reverse Discrimination*

In an important affirmative action decision in *Ricci v. DeStefano*, 129 S.Ct. 2658 (2009), a bare majority reversed an appellate court's ruling upholding a New Haven, Connecticut, decision to disregard test scores for promotions of firefighters because no African Americans passed the tests and the city feared a discrimination lawsuit under Section VII of the Civil Rights Act of 1964 for using a test that had a "disparate impact" on minorities. The city was sued by white firefighters who passed the test but were denied promotions. Writing for the Court, Justice Kennedy avoided a Fourteenth Amendment equal protection challenge and ruled narrowly on statutory grounds that under Section VII employees must have a "strong basis in evidence" that a test is deficient and discriminatory, rather than just "raw racial statistics." Justice Kennedy observed that, "The process was open and fair. . . . The problem, of course, is that after the tests were completed, the raw racial results became the predominant rationale for the city's refusal to certify the results. . . . Fear of litigation [brought by minorities] alone cannot justify an employer's reliance on race to the detriment of individuals who passed the examinations and qualified for promotions." Concurring Justice Scalia, however, added that "The war between disparate impact and equal protection will be waged sooner or later, and it behooves us to begin thinking about how—and on what terms—to make peace between them." By contrast, writing for dissenting Justices Stevens, Souter, and Breyer, Justice Ginsburg countered that "Congress and, until the decision just announced, this Court regarded Title VII's dual prescriptions on intentional and disparate impact as complementary. . . . Standing on equal footing, both provisions aim to end workplace discrimination and promote genuinely equal opportunity."

D | Nonracial Classifications and the Equal Protection of the Law

(4) Alienage and Age

■ THE DEVELOPMENT OF LAW

Recent Rulings on Age Discrimination

CASE	VOTE	RULING
Gomez-Perez v. Potter, Postmaster General, 128 S.Ct. 1931 (2008)	6:3	Writing for the Court, Justice Alito held that under the Age Discrimination in Employment Act federal employees may not be

subjected to retaliation because of their complaints about age discrimination. Chief Justice Roberts and Justices Thomas and Scalia dissented.

CBOCS West v. Humphries, 128 S.Ct. 1951 **(2008)**	7:2	Writing for the Court, Justice Breyer held that employment-related retaliation claims are per-

missible under Title VII of the Civil Rights Act of 1964. Humphries had alleged that CBOCS terminated his employment because he is black and had complained that a black co-worker was also dismissed based on race. Justice Thomas and Scalia dissented.

Gross v. FBL Financial Services, Inc., 129 S.Ct. 2343 **(2009)**	7:2	Writing for the Court, Justice Thomas held that age, by a preponderance of evidence, must be the "but for" cause of adverse em-

ployment action under the Age Discrimination Employment Act of 1967 (ADEA). In doing so, Justice Thomas made clear that companies may not be held to age discrimination suits of mixed motives because (1) that standard had proven over the years difficult to articulate to juries, and (2) even though Congress has extended mixed motive standards to many disparate treatment claims, it failed to do so with respect to age discrimination. Justices Stevens, Souter, Ginsburg, and Breyer dissented.

INDEX OF CASES

Cases printed in boldface are excerpted on the page(s) printed in boldface.

Other Books by David M. O'Brien

Storm Center:
The Supreme Court in American Politics
8th ed.

Constitutional Law and Politics:
Vol. 1. *Struggles for Power and Governmental Accountability*
Vol. 2. *Civil Rights and Civil Liberties*
7th ed.

Animal Sacrifice and Religious Freedom:
Church of Lukumi Babalu Aye v. City of Hialeah

To Dream of Dreams:
Religious Freedom and Constitutional Politics in Postwar Japan

Judicial Roulette

What Process Is Due?
Courts and Science-Policy Disputes

The Public's Right to Know:
The Supreme Court and the First Amendment

Privacy, Law, and Public Policy

Judges on Judging: Views from the Bench
3rd ed. (editor)

The Lanahan Readings on Civil Rights aqnd Civil Liberties
3rd ed. (editor)

Abortion and American Politics
(with Barbara H. Craig)

Judicial Independence in the Age of Democracy:
Critical Perspectives from Around the World
(edited with Peter Russell)

The Politics of Technology Assessment:
Institutions, Processes and Policy Disputes
(edited with Donald Marchand)

Views from the Bench:
The Judiciary and Constitutional Politics
(edited with Mark Cannon)

The Politics of American Government
3d ed.
(with Stephen J. Wayne, G. Calvin Mackenzie, and Richard Cole)

Government by the People
22nd ed.
(with David B. Magleby, Paul Light, James MacGregor Burns,
J. W. Peltason, and Thomas E. Cronin)

Courts and Judicial Policymaking
(with Christopher Banks)